The Light Must Be Perfect

'Placing the Canadian Colours on Wolfe's Monument
in Westminster Abbey'.
1917. Oil on canvas. 98½ x 47½ cm.
Courtesy of Archives Canada, Picture Division, Ottawa.

Mount Edith Cavell, Alberta.
c. 1922. Watercolour. 32 x 25 cm.
'The brilliance of alpine uplands sparkling with millions of flowers',
Emily Warren, 1922.
Courtesy of Helen Simpson Lynett, Toronto.
Unless otherwise noted,
all paintings reproduced in this book are watercolours.

The Light Must Be Perfect

THE LIFE AND ART OF

Emily Warren

A BIOGRAPHICAL MEMOIR BY
CONSTANCE McRAE

DREADNAUGHT

Published with the assistance of
THE CANADA COUNCIL
THE ONTARIO ARTS COUNCIL
WINTARIO

Designed and produced at
DREADNAUGHT
24 Sussex Avenue, Toronto Canada

The text was typeset by Paramount Typesetting.
Colour separations by Imperial Graphics.
The plates printed by Delgraphics.
The binding by Martin Bookbinding.
The text was printed
offset at University of Toronto Press
using linotype Primer and handset Century Schoolbook types,
in a second edition of 750 copies,
January 1982.

Contents

Preface

The title of this book, *The Light Must Be Perfect*, is a phrase of Emily Warren's that expresses her dedication as a painter to the precise rendering of light's effects, both in nature and in architecture, which she regards as humanity's most concerted attempt to express its own deepest nature. Light is not only subject but also theme and inspiration in her paintings. In an extraordinarily coherent life's work, she unwaveringly interpreted the appearances of light on certain types of subjects throughout Canada, Great Britain and Western Europe.

When she was only thirteen years old, in a bold move to achieve her already strong ambition to become an important artist, Warren wrote for guidance to England's great art critic and philosopher, John Ruskin. Ruskin, then about to retire from his chair at Oxford, undertook to teach her himself, and directed her artistic development for the next five years. Naturally, then, his study of light effects, especially those of Turner, had a permanent influence on her. But the spiritual and moral meanings she expresses through light are her own, though they resemble and must have been encouraged by Ruskin's beliefs. An exuberant yet calm confidence and joy in life emerges not only from her paintings, but from her own words in conversations, letters and journals, and perhaps most of all from the evidence of her life.

Warren's impressive knowledge of geology, botany and architecture was the result of extensive academic work and of experience derived from a gruelling routine which she imposed on herself throughout an active career of over fifty years. Her technique, equal or superior to that of other painters working in Canada during her Canadian phase (1919–1956), sprang from thorough absorption of the best art education available in late nineteenth-century England. Yet this training never dominated or deadened an inspiration fostered by her own strong-willed nonconformity and the example of a great teacher.

By her mid-twenties, Warren had established a successful career in an exclusively male preserve, architectural painting. Throughout her life she was a professional painter, often a commission painter. After she had come to Canada, she was one of the very few artists of her time, male or female, able to earn a living by art without doing commercial work. She was a Royal Academician and a member of the Royal Society of British Artists; in 1939, when she had been twenty years in her adopted Canada, the latter body made her a Fellow – a signal honour then limited to thirteen living artists at any one time.

Given the eminence of her artistic mentor, the quantity and quality of her accomplishment, and the honours she received, why has she disappeared so completely that no history or catalogue of Canadian painting now mentions her? In *The Light Must Be Perfect*, Constance McRae suggests several reasons, including Warren's style, which was associated with influences that artists aiming at a national Canadian modernism were eager to repudiate. Yet, in retrospect, we can clearly see that Ruskin's doctrine of the local character of all good landscape painting, influential in Canada, is strongly exemplified by her Canadian works and should have made her an ally, not a bystander, in the movements of the 1920s and 1930s.

Whatever the causes of her isolation from the artistic community in Canada, it was a fact that meant her work was not acquired by public galleries and other influential collections. Consequently, the paintings vanished into the homes of private buyers, where they have remained.

Constance McRae, a friend of Warren's from the painter's arrival in 1919, has produced a vivid portrait by drawing upon her own recollections, the direct testimony of other Warren acquaintances, and many letters and diaries. Not a full-scale biography, Mrs McRae's book is something perhaps even more interesting and valuable: a rare example of a memoir motivated by affection that is crisp and unadorned, conveying its subject through fact with a minimum of editorial or emotional comment. Here Emily Warren emerges as a talented, courageous and generous person, beset with troubles yet sustained by a powerful trust in both life and artistic creativity. Though she was thwarted in many things, ultimately she was successful – her paintings are one proof, and this book is another. It testifies to the impact on all who knew her of her personality and her deep commitment to human betterment through art, and conveys that force to a new generation.

A.F. MORITZ
Toronto Canada
March 1981

Introduction

Bah! What's fame? Only a fancied life in others' breath!
EMILY WARREN, 1951

In September 1919 I moved to Ottawa to take up duties with the Department of Soldiers' Civil Re-establishment and took a room at the Ottawa Ladies' College, which rented a few rooms to professional women. My first morning at the college I had planned to have breakfast downtown before reporting to work. I was hesitant to confront so many inquisitive faces. There came a knock at my door, and to my great surprise, breakfast appeared on a tray carried by a middle-aged, rather heavily built lady, who I supposed could be no other than the wife of the caretaker.

'Saw you come in last night and we do this for everyone – no trouble at all.' Then with a friendly smile she vanished. That was how I met Emily Warren, and from that moment on my interest in her never diminished.

At the time I met her she was forty-nine years old and a prominent, established and respected English artist. Raised under strict Victorian discipline, she had nevertheless been able to assert herself and her determination to paint. Credit for developing her talent when she was young was due to John Ruskin, England's foremost art critic at that time. In fifty-five letters of encouragement and gentle criticism, he guided her early efforts. She furthered her education by attending night classes, and she graduated from the Royal College of Art, South Kensington, at the age of eighteen. At the same time she pursued architectural studies, and by her early thirties she was acclaimed one of Great Britain's finest painters of architectural subjects and was basking in the sunshine of important patronage.

She had arrived in Canada only a few weeks before we met, bringing with her two large paintings, entitled 'Canada's Tribute'. They depict the placing of the Canadian colours on Wolfe's monument in Westminster Abbey, and are based on a scene which she actually observed while painting the interior architecture of the Abbey one day during World War I. However, the paintings were partly imaginary and ideal, too, in that they included the regimental colours and portraits of all the commanders of the Canadian Expeditionary Force – an inclusiveness that had been enjoined upon her by the Canadian War Office in London when she sought its authorization to paint a version of the scene that had stirred her imagination and sympathies. She had begun the paintings in 1917 and brought them to Ottawa to finish and arrange for sale. Warren was not a good business-woman. Due to the urgency of the struggle in 1917, the formality of a written contract had been overlooked. Then, when Prime Minister Sir Robert Borden, who had promised that the government would buy the paintings, was unable to arrange their purchase because of ill health, she became entangled in Ottawa's web of political manoeuvring and controversy. It was twenty-seven years before the government finally bought the paintings, and then the price only covered some of her expenses.

The 'Canada's Tribute' paintings, though her largest in scale and conception, are basically atypical in the career of an artist who was one of her era's leaders in the interpretation of landscape and architecture, but who rarely painted the human figure or narrative and patriotic subjects. However, they assume enormous importance in her biography. They brought her to Canada, which she adopted enthusiastically as her own country and in which she found abundant new inspiration for her Turneresque genius in expressing light, colour and the clear forms that underlie the shifting, indefinite details of nature. Further, her long, frustrating struggle to find some official place for 'Canada's Tribute' among Canada's memorials to those who served in wartime illustrates both Emily Warren's desire to contribute to her society, and the growing isolation, obscurity and economic difficulty that changing fashions in art, artistic rejection of non-native Canadians and lack of acceptance for women as artists all imposed on her during the final, Canadian half of her remarkable career.

Despite her frustration over the sale of the paintings, her first year in Canada was exhilarating. She was far from her family and able to live as she liked. She was captivated by the autumn colours around Ontario and Quebec – they stimulated her eye for the combination of light and colour, her greatest artistic strength. Not long after her arrival she travelled west and was equally impressed by the Rocky Mountains. She, like Ruskin, had a great passion for studying mountains, and in fact her geological knowledge was extensive. She also found that Canada's drier climate suited her; she suffered far less from bronchitis.

That year she began the pattern she was to continue for the rest of her life. She would leave Canada in late March or early April to travel to England and paint the spring flowers. Then much of the summer would be spent sketching there and on the Continent. Late in August or early in September she would return to Ottawa – she felt compelled to be back for the fall leaves.

She crossed Canada many times, from St. John's to Victoria, lecturing and sketching. When her British passport expired in 1929, she applied for and received a Canadian one. In 1947, her status as a Canadian citizen was confirmed by the Canadian Citizenship Act. But in Canada she was generally regarded as English, and her adoptive country has overlooked her accomplishments. My friendship with her grew during the 1920s and the 1930s, the years of her greatest productivity in Canada; and during the 1940s and until her death in 1956, I continued to be in close touch with her.

Her personality was singularly impressive, and I saved all the letters that she wrote to me over the years; I wanted to understand what made her look upon life with such a cheerful and philosophical spirit when fate was so unkind. She never forgot her friends, never indulged in regret. Her nature – which seemed free from fault, meanness or resentfulness – is demonstrated in her letters, many of which are published in this book.

Although she was widely known as an important artist outside Canada, no mention of her has ever been made in the many anthologies on the art of her chosen homeland. Why? When I began to collect information about her for this memoir, I went to the library of the National Gallery in Ottawa. My request for her file evoked a blank look on the face of the young librarian until, as I turned to leave, he blurted out, 'Oh, you mean that odd English artist who used to be all around Ottawa!' Had he said 'odd English *woman* artist', I think he would have voiced all the elements that played a part in her exclusion from the Canadian art establishment. She was presumed to be English. She was odd – she refused to live the way most people thought middle-aged women should live, and her appearance and dress were old-fashioned and suited to her work. And she was a woman. Although she was regarded seriously as an artist in England – to give one example, she was elected an Associate of the Royal Society of British Artists in 1913 and a Fellow in 1939 – she was never taken into account by critics in Canada. Perhaps part of the reason, too, is to be found in the fact that her great specialty, architectural painting, was of little interest to the critics or public in such a young country as Canada. Another probable cause was the shift of taste occurring during the 1920s in Canada, as the country enthusiastically embraced the tenets of modern art and sought a specifically Canadian modernism. Formed in both technique and theory by the great mid-Victorian critic-philosopher Ruskin, she represented a strong exponent of high nineteenth-century ideals in a new century that was busy revolting against its upbringing.

Nevertheless, she supported herself by her painting for most of her life, something few Canadian artists were then able to do. Undaunted by the lack of critical support, she applied her own special talent to brighten the lives of people in her adoptive country. During

Campo Santo, Pisa, Italy.
c. 1910. 32 x 42 cm.
Courtesy of the Ruskin Galleries, Bembridge School, Isle of Wight, UK.

Dawn, Kensington High Street, London.
c. 1915. 23 x 18 cm.
One of a portfolio of sketches presented by Emily Warren to decorate the
messrooms of Canadian troops training at Witley Camp
during World War I.
Courtesy of Miss Louise Hill, Fredericton, New Brunswick.

her arduous itineraries abroad, she travelled third class and worked hard to paint beautiful and historical places for the pleasure of Canadians trapped by the Depression. In seventeen summers, she created a scholarly repertoire of many illustrated lectures, which she used to entertain Canadians from coast to coast in churches, schools, hotel ballrooms or Women's Institute meetings in farm kitchens.

While clouds sometimes darkened her personal affairs, her Turner-like gift of depicting light never failed to illuminate her thousands of paintings. With great care she selected the hour of day and season of year that displayed to the finest advantage the form, colour and chiaroscuro of an edifice. Her paintings were veritable works of love. Two Ruskin museums in England, on the Isle of Wight and at Brant-wood in the Lake District, have important paintings from her earlier work. Canada has the only comprehensive record of the second half of her career in the form of the Warren Collection in the Thomas Fisher Rare Book Library of the University of Toronto. Her output was prodigious; for example, in the summer of her eightieth year she did sixty-six sketches. In a working life of over six decades she must have completed an enormous number of paintings, but thus far few have ever come onto the market; they are treasured by the families of those that bought them at her solo exhibitions in Ottawa or at sales in private homes. The relative anonymity that was Emily Warren's lot in the second half of her career has prolonged itself, because her paintings were not written about and bought in public, but disappeared into private collections, where most of them still remain.

Testimonials of Emily Warren's force of character have come to me from scores of her friends, and have reinforced my conviction that only a great person could project such an image. That particular aura would have been forgotten, as her paintings have been, had it not been for the encouragement of these friends and the help given by the media. Thomas Norrington, when vice-chancellor of Oxford University, convinced me that a biography of Emily Warren should be written because of her training under and knowledge of John Ruskin. J.S. Dearden, curator of the two Ruskin Museums in England, furnished me with the information on file there. Elizabeth Bartlet obtained vital statistics for me from Somerset House, London. The editors of the *Canadian Collector Magazine*, the late Jack Tracy of the Canadian Press, Kay Kritzwiser of the Toronto *Globe and Mail*, and the Ottawa *Evening News* program of the CBC provided the necessary publicity to locate many hundreds of paintings. Photographers Joseph Scott of Ottawa, Lloyd Dingle of Toronto and Judy Kavanagh of Fredericton contributed their skill to create an extraordinary catalogue of the paintings in the form of colour slides. These are destined to go into the Warren Collection but are still in the process of being collected. Daisy Kennedy, RN, of Dunrobin,

Ontario preserved Ruskin's drawings for the Warren Collection, as well as Ruskin letters which are, following the wish of the artist, now in the Ruskin Museum at Bembridge School, Isle of Wight. Dr Lorne MacLachlan, DDS, of Ottawa saved Emily Warren's unique lantern slides. Editor Mary McD Maude revised the original manuscript. Finally, Albert Moritz of Dreadnaught contributed a Preface and, in the concluding chapter, traced the intellectual link between Emily Warren and the doctrine of John Ruskin. He also guided the book through the various stages of production.

To all of the above, I am deeply grateful.

Mary Warren, née Gifford, Emily's mother.

Emily's father, Matthew Henry Warren,
a former British naval officer who became
connected with the development of Canadian fisheries.

Emily Mary Bibbens Warren, RA, RBA. 1869–1956.
Photographed in 1920 by Horsdahl, Ottawa.

CHAPTER I

A Perfect Unsurpassable Eye for Colour

The origin of art is imitation touched with delight; delight, that is to say, in God's work not in man's own.
JOHN RUSKIN to Emily Warren
Circa 1885

On her mother's side, Emily Warren was descended from one of the oldest families in England, the Giffords. There were 'Giffards' (the original spelling) among the Crusaders and an early Giffard chantry had been built. The many Giffords recorded in the Wiltshire village of Ashton-Gifford were accounted ancestors by the family in Emily Warren's time.

Emily's maternal great-grandfather was Edward Gifford, who is said to have married a maid of honour at the royal court, though her name is lost to family tradition. His son, also Edward, was an architect and a close friend of the Duke of Kent, Queen Victoria's father. Edward's wife, née Janet Johnston, bore him four daughters and three sons; the oldest child, Mary Gifford, was Emily's mother. One of the sons, Algernon, became an Anglican priest and held a temporary charge in Newfoundland, before going to Oamaru, New Zealand, where he made his career. His brief stay in Canada later became the direct occasion of his sister Mary's meeting her future husband. Of Mary Gifford's other siblings, Edward was an architect like his father, and became a Royal Academician.

Emily's father, Matthew Henry Warren, was born about 1820, the son of Matthew Warren, a merchant. He was given the education of the English upper classes, including a tour of the Continent accompanied by a tutor. According to family tradition, he had been heir to a sizable estate, but had renounced it in favour of a brother who wanted to marry but did not have the means. Matthew entered the navy and is said to have survived several shipwrecks during his service. His duty took him several times to Newfoundland, and he decided to settle there, which he eventually did, becoming part owner of a fleet of Newfoundland schooners that carried codfish to Europe and the United States.

Matthew Warren must have become closely involved in life in St. John's and studied the fishery carefully. Early in 1853, he gave a lecture on the Newfoundland fisheries at the St. John's Mechanics' Institute, later regarded as something of a classic.[1] It was at St. John's that Matthew met the beautiful Mary Gifford, destined to be his wife. Emily explained: 'My uncle, the Reverend Algernon Gifford went to Newfoundland and took my mother to be a companion to his young bride. One day my mother saw a young man leaning over the gate of the rectory – it was Matthew Warren.' Their romance culminated in marriage at the Anglican parish church of St. Stephen, Westminster, on 12 March 1856.

Their first years of marriage were spent in Canada, where Matthew pursued a business as a commission merchant. Their first daughter, Annie, was born in Quebec City. Elizabeth Janet (Bessie) was born in Montreal, and Ada Matilda was born after their return to Newfoundland. Matthew's increasingly poor health forced his retirement and return to England, and Louisa Ann (Louie) was born in Earls Court, London. For a short time the family occupied the house on Doughty Street where Charles Dickens had lived, and then settled in Exeter, Devon.

Emily was born on 20 October 1869 in the Exeter parish of Bradninch, which consisted of only eight houses. She was given the name of her godmother, Emily Mary Bibbens, who died when the child was only two years of age, leaving her £800 per year and a home on the south coast of England. The legacy was contested, however, and although it later paid for Emily to be sent to school, by the time she was fourteen the estate had been taken up by the costs of litigation.

Emily's early years were spent at Larkbeare House near the River Exe in a pleasant area, but her memories of that period were bitter. 'When you are the youngest of five girls in a Victorian household, the odds are staked against you from the day of your birth.' She was dominated by her older sisters, but she showed her determination early. At age five or six she wrote to Queen Victoria for 'a change in the laws' when punished for not keeping her shelf in the nursery cupboard tidy. (It was not until she was twenty-one that she discovered that the letter – lacking a proper stamp – had been given to her father.) She recalled that English children were not allowed to speak spontaneously or to go out alone. Whenever she managed to escape and to meet neighbours or explore her surroundings, her family would soon come looking for her. As an outlet for creative energy and as a means of expression, she turned to painting. 'In my silent prayers I used to thank God because my brushes didn't squeak.' Her mother criticized the amount of time she spent over her brushes, but she was allowed to continue.

---

1. Matthew H. Warren, *Lecture on Newfoundland and its Fisheries delivered by Matthew H. Warren, before the Mechanics' Institute at St. John's, 14th March 1853* (St. John's, Newfoundland, 1853).

A Family of Artists.
c. 1876.
Each person pictured painted her own face;
it is not known which painted the bulk of the picture.
Left to right: Emily, Ada, Louie, Bessie, Annie and Mary (mother).
At this date the father was on the south coast suffering from tuberculosis.

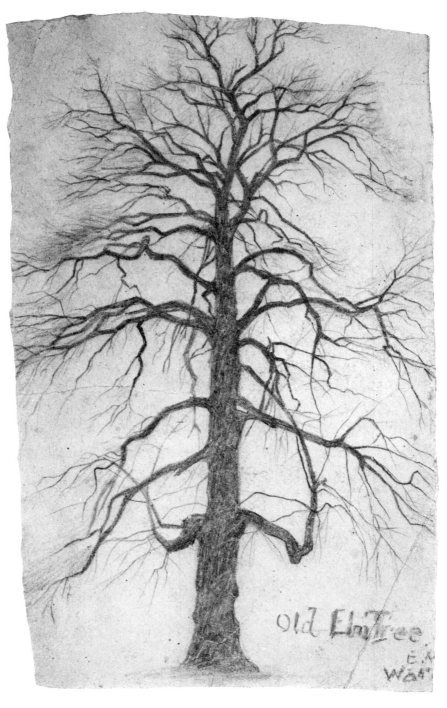

'Old Elm Tree'.
Juvenile sketch by Emily Warren for Ruskin.

Emily's life changed abruptly when her father – the only member of the family she thought understood her – died on 24 September 1879. His partners, through an unscrupulous solicitor, had cheated him, and not long after he developed tuberculosis. With most of his money gone, he was heartbroken at leaving so little to his family. In fact he died bankrupt, with his last assets being taken by the grocery firm of Peters and Hamblin. Little or no help was forthcoming from the Warren family at that time, and Mary now found herself in dire trouble. She could see no alternative but to move to London where her older daughters might find teaching employment, the only occupation open to them.

All five of the Warren daughters were artistic. Annie, the oldest, was the only one to marry. She married Henry Vaughan, a typical English gentleman whom they all adored, and continued to live with the family. Annie was not well liked by Emily, who thought her tyrannical, but she did lovely carvings (including, at a later date, carved wooden frames for Emily's paintings). Bessie, the second daughter, went to art college in St. Petersburg, Russia, where she lived with one of her father's sisters who had married a German admiral at that time living in St. Petersburg. The third sister, Ada, painted interiors and wrote poetry. Her specialty was cathedrals but she also painted from visions, and prints of these works were widely distributed. One such painting depicted a procession of White Knights riding up Dartmoor. In the foreground a blue-robed figure of the Mother of Jesus was directing and blessing their crusade. (Other works by Emily's sisters are reported still to be in churches in England.) Ada taught as well and became the headmistress of Grey Coat School in Westminster. Louie too studied art abroad. She went to Italy for her studies and lived with another of her father's sisters who was married to an Italian colonel. She had a preference for mystical figures and animals in her art. Both Bessie and Louie taught elementary school in London.

For Emily the move to London was an advantage because she was to go to school, a first step toward liberation. A ward-in-chancery, she was sent by her trustees out of London to Malden Girls School for Boarders. Here she spent the next few years relatively happily. She had always been fascinated by history, and had learned the history of Greece and the geography of Asia Minor as a young child by reenacting the ancient battles under the tutelage of her governess. Now she began to read widely in the writings of the important figures of her own time. She read scientist Thomas Huxley's *Evenings through a Microscope* and John Ruskin's *Sesame and Lilies* and *Ethics of the Dust* at school. (In fact, she had read all of Ruskin's works by the time she was fourteen.) A bright child, she was allowed a good deal of freedom at school, or as she put it: 'Usually I "twigged" it somewhat so that I could read what I chose.'

When Emily was thirteen, a medical missionary named Richardson addressed the school on India's need for doctors. Immediately Emily decided to make that her chosen field of labour; her ambition was treated with amused indifference by all the elders in whom she confided. Not easily dissuaded, she sought advice outside the home. From her reading she felt that Ruskin, who was at this time Slade Professor of Fine Art at Oxford,[2] would be the person to whom to write for a sympathetic hearing. Enclosing a card upon which she had painted a branch of heather, she asked if he thought she could ever paint well, but she also told him that she wanted to be a lady doctor and go to India. His answer was written just a few days before her fourteenth birthday.

> *Brantwood,*
> *Coniston, Lancashire*
>
> *84, Woodstock Road*
> *Oxford, 15th Oct. '83*
>
> *My dear little lady*
> *You very certainly may paint much better than 'well', if you like to. But you can't be a paintress and a lady doctor too, for you will soon come to think healing the far nobler and more divine art, and if it is your great wish to be one, – as young as you are – most probably your gift for such work will be great. I can't answer your questions about Dr Richardson etc. this evening but I will find out whatever you want to know for you, – only first please tell me whether you are allowed to have quite your own way in everything? – it isn't every little girl of 13 who has? – May I keep the pretty heath?*
> *Ever affectionately yours,*
>
> *J. Ruskin*

Thus began Emily Warren's relationship with Ruskin and his influence – the dominant one – on her life and work. Ruskin soon came to her home, and according to Emily (who all her life was self-conscious about her appearance) he was disappointed in her, commenting that she stooped. But he advised that she be given training in art for she showed unusual talent. Indeed, two little remnants of sketches, of an old elm tree and a Spanish chestnut, still exist from this very early period and convey an idea of her precocious skill.

During the next few years Ruskin guided Emily's education in art. He told her she should send him everything she did and he would return it with his criticisms. He soon enabled her to begin copying Turner in the British Museum. Then to satisfy Ruskin's strongest

---

2. Ruskin was elected first Slade Professor of Fine Art, Oxford in 1869 (the year of Emily's birth) and resigned the professorship in 1885.

wishes for her, she proceeded to concentrate upon the effects of light. Nowhere were these as beautiful as through the stained glass windows of churches – the right subject for what Ruskin described as 'a perfect unsurpassable eye for colour', in a letter to her dated 30 December 1885.

Darling Emmie
I've found your drawings and have chosen eight of them – they are more beautiful than I thought, and I have the best hopes of your progress and pleasure in your art.

I want you really now to take care of your drawings and to work for sunny landscape – and I hope ever so much from you.

You really have one of the most perfect and pure gifts of colour I ever knew, and I am greatly anxious about you now, and will take all the pains I can with you.

Your work is lovely, *your eye for colour – perfect.*

Coming late home, I find your lovely drawings – most of them are exquisite – You have a perfect unsurpassable eye for colour.

Further training was necessary if she was to pursue such architectural work, and again Ruskin came to her aid. For her first landscape he paid her £30 (then the equivalent of $150), remarking that he had never spent such a sum with so much pleasure. This enabled her to apply for instruction in the class of the eminent architect of the 'British Renaissance' movement, Sir Bannister Fletcher, KC. The application, signed simply E. Warren, was challenged when this young girl of fourteen sought admittance on registration day. Her magic password, the name of Ruskin, soon opened the door. At the end of the year in that class of adults, she qualified for the scholarship but was unable to use it because her family insisted that she now start to earn a living. Thus in 1886 at the age of fifteen she began teaching English and art to the junior pupils at Grey Coat School, which had been started, Emily used to say, by Queen Anne so that girls would have something better to do than to pick blackberries. 'The trouble with teaching,' she told me, 'was that I never had enough daylight for my own painting. I would use my lunch hour to go out and memorize my subject and then try to paint it whenever possible. My greatest delight was to lie on a bank at Kew and study the trees.' Disagreeable as it seemed to her, teaching was essential in order to pay for higher tuition; she was now studying at night at the Royal College of Art, South Kensington. In addition, the discipline teaching imposed was advantageous in preparing her for the lecture platform later on.

Throughout these years, by example and his own drawings, England's greatest living authority on art at that time guided Emily in an exacting yet kindly manner.

He obtained permission for her to sketch in the Museum of Natural History. Today, almost one hundred years later, one can see a watercolour by her in the second-floor mammal gallery: it depicts the gallery as it was in 1888 in full architectural detail. He introduced her to the painter Arthur Severn[3] during one visit to the Museum of Natural History and encouraged her to paint beside Severn at the Institute in Piccadilly. During Emily's sixteenth and seventeenth years, Ruskin also gave her the task of colouring many drawings by Kate Greenaway which he wished to include in one of his books. But after 1889, his reason became permanently clouded, and this illness – of which Emily did not learn until after his death in 1900 – prevented him from ever acknowledging her work.[4]

The highlight of these years for Emily was her visit in 1888 to Ruskin's home on Coniston Water in the Lake District. She had encountered Ruskin at the Museum of Natural History, and he had inquired whether she thought her mother would let her come to Coniston in the holidays for a vacation and to do some landscape sketching and painting. She would have the company of Severn's daughter Lily, who was about the same age. 'As soon as he was gone, I ran every inch of the way home, and breathlessly broke the news that the Professor was to invite me up to Coniston, and would she let me go?' Holidays came at long last and Emily travelled to Windermere by train with Arthur Severn; they were met by his wife and daughter, and driven first to the church to admire the stained glass. Each night of the visit she and Lily dressed in their white frocks to have dessert and wine with Ruskin.

'Brooklet'
Hampton
May 19th 88

Dear Mrs. Severn

I hope you will excuse my not writing to you before to thank both you and Mr. Severn for your very great kindness to my daughter Emmie. I feel I can never be sufficiently grateful to you for all your goodness to her. She will I am sure, as I do, value much the kind instruction Mr. Severn is giving her; and we shall all, as well as Emmie, herself, remember with pleasure her visit to Coniston, and particularly as it is the first time she has been on a visit alone, I am afraid you must find her very shy and awkward. I hope you will not allow her to inconvenience you in any way especially in the length

---

3. Arthur Severn, RI had married Ruskin's cousin, Joan Agnew, in 1871 and they lived with him at Coniston in his declining years and looked after him through his illness.

4. Belleville *Weekly*, 6 January 1921.

84. Woodstock Road
Oxford, 15th Oct '83

Brantwood,
Coniston. Lancashire.

My dear little lady :

You very certainly may paint much better than 'well', if you like to. But you can't be a paintress and a lady doctor too : for you will soon come to think healing the far nobler and more divine art. and if it is your great wish to be one, & so young as you are — most probably your gift for such work will be great. I can't answer your questions about Dr Richardson &c. this evening : but I will find out whatever you want to know for you, — and first please tell me whether you are allowed to have quite your own way in everything ? — it isn't every little girl of 13 who has! — May I keep the pretty heath ?
Ever affectionately yrs :
J Ruskin .

The first of fifty-five letters from Ruskin to Emily Warren.

John Ruskin, 1819–1900, as Emily Warren knew him in 1886:
'poet, painter, art critic and social reformer'.

of her stay; as she now knows the journey I shall feel quite happy in
her coming home alone should you not know of any one coming to
London about the time of her return. Again thanking you very much
for your great kindness.

I am yours faithfully
Mary Warren[5]

At the age of eighteen Emily graduated from the Royal College of
Art. Her thesis with several drawings in ink was 'The Cathedral of
Christ Church, Canterbury; a life history and description'. A photographic memory won first prize for her in a competition at the
college. Anyone familiar with her contest assignment, the High
Street, Oxford, would agree that such a difficult architectural scene
required extraordinary powers.

Her formal education did not end at this point, however. Over the
next few years, to round out her knowledge of subjects necessary for
her career as an artist, she took certificates in biology, botany and
geology at the College of Science, South Kensington. She continued
to feel her lack of formal training in architecture and over the next
decade or more pursued her studies until she was accredited in
architecture, though family tradition does not preserve the nature of
her degree nor from where it was granted.

All her life Emily felt restrained by her family, none of whom she
thought understood her. She shared her father's love of adventure,
love of the unknown, and she could not understand why her mother
and older sisters put obstacles in her path instead of encouraging
her. 'Everything I wanted to do they said I would bitterly regret';
nevertheless her loyalty to them never faltered.

In her late teens and twenties she was closely guarded and denied
the freedom that she felt essential to her spirit. She told me of an
instance when she attended an art congress in Venice at the age of
twenty-one. There were about forty-five Britishers out of a hundred
or so at the congress. 'Annie and Henry were sent to guard me. They
watched my every move like a mouse. If anyone gave me an invitation, it meant certain imprisonment, for I was ordered to go to my
room and stay there. There were several I should like to have talked
to but I had no opportunity. Bannister Fletcher asked if he might
come to see me in London, but I dared not risk what they would say.
Just think, I might have been Lady B.F.,' she said laughingly. Although she might chafe under the restrictions, she was unable to go
against all the dictates of society at that time and rebel against her
family.

During this period, though, she was perfecting her craft. She and
Louie (who had been prevented by her mother from marrying the

---

5. By courtesy of Ruskin Galleries, Bembridge School, Isle of Wight,
England.

man of her choice, a relative of Earl Grey, and attributed to this the indigestion and ill health she suffered for the rest of her life) would go to various cathedral towns in England when school term ended. Emily would paint and Louie would seek relief through religious meditation. They were never without their religious books, which the girls called 'cats' in order to keep them secret. Ada, who also painted cathedral interiors, would sometimes accompany them. Their first such trip was to Canterbury, which Emily studied for her thesis. Ada chose York as her topic. Soon, however, their travels were taking them to the Continent. Italy and Switzerland were loved by Emily as they had been by Ruskin, but Belgium, Holland and France were also visited frequently. The cathedral at Chartres, because of its beautiful stained glass, was a favourite.

Emily Warren always concentrated on colour and the effects of light, whether she was painting in the Swiss Alps or in a cathedral with the sunlight filtering through stained glass. Conditions had to be perfect for her cathedral watercolours – the right time of day and the right season of the year. On occasion she would begin a painting and then have to wait until the following year when light conditions would be the same before finishing it. A perfectionist, she felt compelled always to sketch on location despite her remarkable visual memory. Thus the amount she was able to accomplish in a day was sometimes quite limited, and she would often be up and painting very early if morning light was called for.

Emily's work soon began attracting public notice and selling quite well. A number of prominent people purchased her paintings, which also helped bring attention to her. In 1903, Queen Alexandra purchased a painting of the interior of St. George's Chapel, Windsor, as a present for Edward VII. Emily later sold paintings to Queen Mary, the Duke and Duchess of Argyle and the Duke of Connaught, to name just a few of her prominent supporters. On 2 September 1905, England's distinguished paper the *Queen* featured her work in the art section and reproduced four of her cathedral paintings. Referring to her as 'one of our best painters of architectural subjects', A.F. Morris praised her knowledge of perspective and feeling for tone and colour and commented: 'Perhaps her faculty for indicating the minutest details without any stippling or hardness of outline is one of her best points.'[6]

At about this time her watercolours were bringing in enough money to enable her to give up teaching. She devoted some attention to devising a suitable memorial of her own to Ruskin, who had died in 1900 after a ten-year illness. Emily finally decided that a book should be published which would document his surroundings and

6. A.F. Morris, 'The World of Art: Famous Women Workers, Emily M.B. Warren', *Queen, the Lady's Newspaper* (London), 2 September 1905.

The Choir, St. George's Chapel, Windsor.
Exhibited at the Royal Academy, 1913.
Dimensions, medium and present whereabouts unknown.
Reproduced from a photograph in *The Queen*, 2 September 1905.
Another of Warren's views of this subject, showing the rose window,
was purchased by Queen Alexandra for King Edward VII;
the chapel was the scene of their marriage in 1863.

Tomb of Ilaria di Caretto at Lucca, Italy.
c. 1911. 28 x 42 cm.
Private collection.

show all lovers of beauty the scenes and shrines that he liked best. She would do the illustrations, and Edward T. Cook, the noted journalist and expert on Ruskin, agreed to write the text. Three years of work – 1910 through 1912 – went into the illustrations. Cook later commented that he had merely 'written around her splendid pictures'.[7]

First Emily reread the thirty-nine volumes of Ruskin's writings and then she planned her itinerary. Ruskin had been so enraptured by Italian art that she spent many months in Italy. Her 'Campo Santo, Pisa', was a faultless example of her perspective and light. Now in the Ruskin Museum at Brantwood, it is a permanent record of that building which was all but destroyed by the Nazis in World War II. Another good example of her Italian work is a picture of a white marble tomb of Ilaria di Caretto by Quercia at Lucca. This was Ruskin's favourite piece of statuary and his ideal of Christian sculpture, and he had written eloquently of it in the second volume of *Modern Painters*.[8] After Italy she turned her attention to Switzerland, accompanied this time by Ada. At one point when she was immobilized by an accident to her leg, she had a vision of the Jungfrau and the Castle of Manfred. 'As I was painting and imagining what I had seen the day before, a cloud came over that peak. It was the only illustration in the book which was not done on the spot.' Many of the illustrations were of England, including Ruskin's favourite home, Brantwood, which forms the frontispiece.

She had chosen Ruskin's publishers, George Allen and Company, to publish the book, and she submitted one hundred pictures to them and to Cook for selection. Of these, forty-four were used, twenty-eight in full colour. In December 1912, there was an exhibition of the original drawings for the book at the Dudley Galleries, London. Fifteen hundred copies of the book, titled *Homes and Haunts of John Ruskin*, were printed but shortly afterwards the publisher went bankrupt.[9] Three hundred of these went to the United States. Emily Warren's own copy is in the Ottawa Public Library, and there are copies in the University of Toronto Rare Book Library and the Metropolitan Toronto Library. Neither she nor E.T. Cook was paid anything for the work. 'Fortunately, I did not do it for money,' she told me.

While she was working on the memorial she went to see an exhibition of art at the Institute in Piccadilly and ran into Mrs Arthur

---

7. Ottawa *Citizen*, 23 September 1923.

8. John Ruskin, *Modern Painters* Vol. II (London, 1888), page 76.

9. E.T. Cook, *Homes and Haunts of John Ruskin with twenty-eight illustrations in colour from original drawings and sixteen in black and white by E.M.B. Warren* (London: George Allen & Company, 1912).

Severn, who invited her to visit the Severn family, whom she had not seen for twenty years. 'Of course, I went, and, crossing the threshold, Mrs Severn clasped a most beautiful necklace about my neck. That necklace was comprised of a brooch and earrings which belonged to Ruskin's mother and Ruskin's watch chain.' It was her most prized possession and is now at Brantwood.

Her travels did not cease with the book's publication. A love of adventure – and perhaps of danger – kept her travelling all her life. And certainly she had many adventures while illustrating *Homes and Haunts*, including a narrow escape from death when a boulder just missed her on a narrow path at Wegenalp in Switzerland. On one occasion in Holland, when she was having her fortune told, a gypsy informed her that she had psychic powers that should be developed. She later would use this gift to tell fortunes in Canada to raise money for the Red Cross and to entertain her friends; throughout her life she maintained a serious interest in thought transference. Her travels to the Continent were interrupted by the outbreak of war in 1914; she was in fact leading a class of adults in Switzerland at the time and managed to shepherd them safely back to England through France.

In each of the years 1910 to 1912 during which she was working on the Ruskin memorial she had paintings accepted by the Royal Academy, but they were not shown because of lack of space. In 1913, however, she had two accepted and shown. The first, 'Interior of St. George's Chapel, Windsor', was a subject that inspired her brush more than once; the beauty of the carving, the difficult fan tracery roof, the rich gleam of colour imparted by the banners of the Knights of the Garter and the light through the stained-glass windows seemed enhanced by her rendering. The second painting, 'The Choir of St. Paul's', was an outstanding example of her knowledge of perspective. She loved St. Paul's and painted the majestic dome in many moods – seen from Fleet Street of a winter's morning as a faint silver round against a pale sky, from the Thames at sunset, or from St. Paul's Cross in the misty gold and green of her favourite season, spring.

From the day that Ruskin wrote to Emily saying, 'I only wish I could do myself what you can do now', she resolved never to be influenced by any other artist. She vowed to develop to the full any talent with which she had been blessed, for the glorification of God's handiwork, and to ask for no other reward. Thus her style became strictly individual and remained consistent throughout her career; her paintings can be recognized immediately. Because she was sent to copy Turner for colour and light effects, she was capable of creating the atmospheric nuances strikingly noticeable in many of her cathedral interiors.

In 1913, she became an associate of the Royal Society of British Artists, but her progress through the English art establishment prior

The Wetterhorn as seen from Burglauenen near Grindelwald, Switzerland.
From *Homes and Haunts of John Ruskin*.

Sir Robert Borden.
June 1920. 27 x 20 cm.
Courtesy of the Canada War Museum, Ottawa.

to that date is harder to establish. Her signature on the fly leaf of her mother's copy of *Homes and Haunts of John Ruskin* indicates that she used her title RA (Royal Academician) as early as 1912, while another signature on an old sheet of notepaper, also using the title, suggests a still earlier date. In 1913, the ARBA (Associate of the Royal Society of British Artists) title was conferred. Finally, in 1939, after she had made her home in Ottawa for twenty years, the Royal Society of British Artists notified her that she had been awarded a Fellowship, an outstanding honour then limited to thirteen artists at any given time. She told no one, but to satisfy her personal pride, she had her title on the brochures to her lectures updated to read 'RBA'.

She was also a member of the British Water Colour Society, the Old Dudley Arts Society, the Society of Women Artists and the Aberdeen Society of Art. She was elected to both of the latter in 1913. She was very active on the committee of the Society for the Preservation of Memorials in London and made a comprehensive record in pictures of London's famous old buildings. Also on the committee was Walter Godfrey of the Royal Institute of British Architects, who collected the architectural details. Hence those buildings that were bombed during the war could be rebuilt exactly as they had been. She was, of course, a steadfast worker for Ruskin Societies, following their activities with great interest. These varied pursuits provided a good foundation on which to build prestige as a lecturer in the second half of her career.

CHAPTER II

'Canada's Tribute' Comes to Canada

Of every fifty endeavours throughout my life, scarcely one has succeeded.
EMILY WARREN, 1942

In 1917, Warren was working on a study in oils of a scene in the interior of Henry VII Chapel, Westminster (which was later acquired by Queen Mary), when the stillness was disturbed by a Canadian regimental colour party. Curiosity impelled her to inquire of the verger the cause of the commotion. He explained that a detachment of about twenty men from a Canadian infantry regiment had arrived for the placing of their regimental colours, which were to be deposited for safekeeping in the hallowed precincts of Westminster Abbey before the unit went on its way to the battlefields. At the mention of Canada she abandoned her painting to watch the ceremonial. The party she watched was led by Captain Harold Riley of Calgary, later killed in action.

The soft organ music, the khaki uniforms of those sturdy men, the gentle rays of summer sunlight, which filtered through the multi-coloured windows diffusing the light on the surfaces of the Wolfe monument, provided a scene that she could not dismiss from her thoughts. It reminded her of a request made by a cousin, Major Jack Sweet, a Vancouver lawyer and the son of Archdeacon Sweet of Victoria, British Columbia and grandson of Evelina Gifford Vial, one of the sisters of Warren's mother. He had been staying with his friend, broadcaster and journalist Max Aitken (later Lord Beaverbrook), before going to the front with the Seaforth Highlanders, and he had asked if at some time she would paint his regimental flag. Jack had been killed just a short time before in the battle of Vimy Ridge, one of over ten thousand Canadian casualties.

All these thoughts aroused Warren's emotions so much that she at once resolved to divert her entire energy to painting an historical scene for Canada, whose voluntary contribution was so much appreciated. Her painting must interpret this moving wartime spectacle in London's great shrine. She immediately told the verger of her plan and was introduced to Captain Riley, who advised her to write to the War Office in London. He felt confident that they would cooperate by providing the names of the people and units needed and might assist her in other ways. While awaiting their reply, Emily Warren recorded the scene which had been so indelibly printed in her memory by making first a watercolour sketch and later a painting in oils.[1]

The high command of the Canadian troops soon learned about Emily Warren's proposition. Lieutenant General Sir Arthur Currie (also a friend of Jack Sweet) and Major General Sir Richard Turner gave instructions that she should have every assistance necessary. The reply from the War Office, on the other hand, would have daunted any other painter. Whether it intended to unnerve her or not, the Office claimed that such an historical record should portray seventy-seven commanders and fifty-two regimental colours. A tall order! Undaunted, she decided to use two 11½ by 6 foot canvasses and call them 'Canada's Tribute'. She imagined a monumental scene in which the men would be arranged around Wolfe's monument watching as the last of the colours were placed there. Colonel H. Willis O'Connor, aide de camp to the commander in chief in the field, helped to arrange the grouping and assisted her in the abbey whenever possible. The Duke of Connaught, Canada's governor general from 1911 to 1916, posed for her in the abbey, then advised her of the proper position to be occupied by the Prince of Wales, who, learning of her difficulties, had his aide de camp, Sir Godfrey Thomas, notify her that he could not sit in London but would sit for her in Ottawa if she were there in August of that year during His Royal Highness' visit to Canada. Unfortunately, Warren was scheduled to lecture in Switzerland, and hence the portraits of the Prince of Wales and that of General M.S. Mercer, who had been killed in June 1916 in the Ypres Salient, were the only portraits in the paintings not actually posed.

With these two exceptions, the portraits were painted from life in a series of short sittings, snatched whenever or wherever the subjects could spare ten or fifteen minutes. She had insisted the War Office guarantee her a ten-minute sitting with each subject, and often she had to go in pursuit of her models.

Then, too, the canvasses had to be shifted before each service, and

---

1. After her arrival in Canada in 1919, the original sketch for the larger canvasses, a watercolour, became the property of Charles A. Bowman, editor of the Ottawa *Citizen*. Sixty-five years later, on the occasion of his grandson's graduation, he presented it to Shawnigan Lake School in British Columbia.

The oil painting, entitled 'Placing the Colours on Wolfe's Monument in Westminster Abbey', was purchased shortly after her arrival in Canada by Sir Arthur Doughty, Dominion Archivist. It may be seen, still in mint condition, in File No. 705-7, Archives Canada, Wellington Street, Ottawa.

with all the extra wartime traffic in the abbey, her task was even more difficult than it might have been. Her cumbersome equipment included a scaffold and ten-foot ladders which had to be set up and taken down again between the frequent services. Throngs of visitors to the abbey, with the Canadians taking special pride and interest, stood in fascination and watched her dream take form from a messy old palette. One veteran in a wheelchair approached to offer a coin in the hope that it might help to buy another brush! She accepted it gracefully, delighted to let him share in the work. The sketching of the flags presented another problem. Regiments did not care to loan them. One day while she was engaged in her work, twelve soldiers, each bearing a regimental flag, approached, informing her that they had been instructed to bring the flags and wait until she sketched them. When she explained that the sketching of one flag would require three to four hours they were somewhat nonplussed. However, the flags were finally left with her, with the exception of that of the Princess Patricia's Canadian Light Infantry which was guarded during the entire sketch. Further complication occurred when one regiment was absorbed into another, or when a temporary flag was replaced by a permanent one after she had painted the former. A greater worry was the disagreement and jostling for position of some of the generals. Moreover, many objected to posing, even for ten minutes. 'I certainly did a lot of running around after generals in those days. They were the hardest people to find, and I simply had to have them in my paintings. If I couldn't find them in the camps, I stalked them in London hotels until I got them to let me sketch their features ... One of them sent me a bill for his photograph.'

When the war ended, the paintings still required further details, so General Currie advised her to take them to Canada. This would mean removing them from their stretchers and having them carefully sealed in zinc-lined airtight metal tubes. Sensing the futility of such an expensive undertaking without any legal commitment, she was cautious enough to consult Lord Beaverbrook. Eventually she was referred to the art adviser for the Canadian War Records Commission, Paul Konody, whose responsibility it was to commission artists to paint for the Canadian War Record. Although he was not prepared to commission her work, he advised her to complete the canvasses and he assured her that no one else would be commissioned to do the same subject – a safe assertion!

She decided then that she would take her canvasses and travel to Canada, but she feared telling her family. When it was time to buy her ticket, she confided in her favourite sister, Ada, but the dreaded family announcement was withheld until just before her departure, in order to mitigate any censure. To her exasperation and amusement Ada sent her off with a whistle and admonishments to use it if she were in any danger.

The sea voyage, and then the drier climate of Ottawa, gave her such a feeling of exhilaration that she entered Canada, land of her future adoption, with high hopes and a sense of roguish independence. She lived briefly at the YWCA until her precious canvasses were set up in the Victoria Memorial Museum, where she completed the final and most exacting work. But the chase was not over; for example, the flag of Calgary's battalion was returned to Alberta before she could get the final details. Being a perfectionist, she felt obliged to pursue it to the west. The last sittings were of Prime Minister Sir Robert Borden, the central figure of one of the groups, in his office at the Parliament Buildings.

Finally the two pictures were finished on 8 June 1920, and as had been arranged, Warren dictated a letter to Borden's secretary offering the paintings to the Canadian government for $10,000. As soon as the House of Commons adjourned, he expected to ensure that the negotiation was completed and the paintings suitably placed. In the interim, he suggested that the painter might like to see her works hanging, and directed them to be moved from his office and hung in the reading room of the House of Commons.

Unfortunately, shortly thereafter, Sir Robert Borden suffered a nervous breakdown and retired from public office. His successor, Arthur Meighen, with so many other things to consider, submitted the matter to a committee, which was responsible for purchasing works of art under the budget provided for the purpose. F.J. Shepherd, a Montreal physician, W.Y. Soper, a prominent Ottawa electrical engineer and Eric Brown, the director of the National Gallery, reviewed the matter, and in 1921 the paintings were summarily rejected; they were 'symbolic, not suitable for purchase by the Gallery'.

It seems clear from contemporary records, as well as testimony from Emily Warren herself and from her friends, that the 'Canada's Tribute' paintings became caught up in Canada's struggle for artistic redefinition as soon as they were deprived of Sir Robert Borden's championship. They were perceived by some as 'patriotic' works (indeed they are so, though Warren's technical mastery makes them more than mere genre paintings) and therefore commendable quite apart from questions of artistic merit; others saw them, apparently, as old-fashioned and European, whether for subject or style or both. Emily Warren herself regarded them as 'of historical rather than artistic value' (see Appendix A). Entering the fray on the side of the paintings, the Ottawa *Citizen* referred (in an article published 27 December 1920, before the board had rejected purchase) in the following terms to the alleged role played in the affair by Paul Konody, and by the shift of Canadian taste toward modernism in general.

It is understood that a certain post-impressionist artist in London, of Hungarian origin, with influence in the Canadian War Records Office, expressed opposition to Miss Warren's work – possibly without ever seeing it. Miss Warren's understanding of art principles is based on the teachings of an English master, John Ruskin. It is the fashion of some ultra-modern artists to affect to despise people like Ruskin. But the battalion colours in Westminster Abbey were not painted to please futurist, cubist or any extreme post-impressionist school of art in London studios. They were painted for Canada.

The artistic climate of the time in Canada was one of change, in which the rising artists sought two things: a complete absorption by Canadian art of the most recent twentieth-century developments, and a wholly Canadian version of this modern idiom with which to express Canadian experience. It was, after all, the period in which the Group of Seven, formed in 1913, began to be noticed and exert influence. In such a climate, some overlooked the timelessness of Emily Warren's art and saw only that it represented England, Ruskin and Victorian principles. Even so, in Europe Warren was used to dealing with people who, if they disagreed with her style, could at least appreciate her skill and authority. It was disillusionment for her to discover that this all-important and powerful committee for selection of war memorials for the National Gallery of Canada would not accept her work.

The committee's decision caused a new war in Ottawa. Ex-servicemen, as well as many generals who had served at the front, supported by the editors of the city's two newspapers, opposed that verdict. General Sir Arthur Currie, commander in chief, wrote to the *Citizen* recommending the paintings be purchased for Canada's historical records. Charles A. Bowman, the editor, championed Warren's cause and even went to the prime minister.[2] Mr Meighen referred him to F.B. McCurdy, minister of public works. McCurdy's excuse was curt: 'They had not been commissioned by the War Records Committee, and in any case the funds of that committee had run out.'

Warren at this point did not know what to do. In an interview with the Ottawa *Citizen* she said, 'They are distinctly Canada's pictures, I painted them for Canada and they are of greater interest to Canadians than anyone else.'[3] She did not want to take them back to England. Newspaper comment at the time was entirely on her side

---

2. The complete story by Charles A. Bowman as reported in the Ottawa *Citizen*, 13 May 1949, can be seen in Appendix B.

3. Ottawa *Citizen*, 23 September 1923.

and full of praise for the paintings. The *Belleville Weekly*, 5 January 1921, said, 'There is such sincere feeling in those wartime paintings – a sense of reverence and spiritual beauty suggesting her own mood – certainly a high attainment. They are noble in treatment; a blaze of colour, not only of the flags but from an upper window, suggests some soundless, stirring harmony – a perfect setting for the rapt expression on the upturned faces in reverent memory for Canada's glorious slain.'

Warren, to show her appreciation to those who had posed or given assistance, had colour reproductions printed by the Montreal *Gazette* which were presented to each officer and to others interested; the cost to her was $2,300.00. Using these reproductions, she then began to seek testimonials in England that might help sell her works. Among others she wrote to Sir David Murray, RA, president of the Royal Institute of Painters in Watercolours, London, and to Burleigh Bruhl, president of the British Watercolour Society. She claimed that both of these men wrote back praising her abilities and the conception and execution of her canvasses. Sir Arthur Severn also replied encouragingly to her, commenting: 'I thought it was very good and true when I saw it in the Abbey and hope it will be bought and remain in Canada.'

The paintings were housed temporarily in the Veterans' Clubhouse in Legion Hall on the orders of Brigadier General J.H. MacBrien. On Christmas night the clubhouse caught fire and was destroyed, but the two huge canvasses were saved. From this time until they were finally purchased in 1947, they were in temporary locations – much of the time under unsuitable atmospheric conditions. The distress this situation caused Warren was acute. Her largest, most ambitious work had failed to earn the appreciation that she had expected. It is true that the horrors of the First World War haunted the memories of most Canadians, and the selection committee certainly bought some of the evidence; but in opposing the wishes of a group of brave men who actually lived through those perils and had come to regard Warren as their champion and friend, the committee caused a blot which the government did not erase for twenty-seven years. Hers was the only pictorial record of the commanding officers and regimental colours of the Canadian Expeditionary Force.

CHAPTER III

Painting and Travel
1919-40

The beauty of this wonderful world is more miraculous than anything man can create.
EMILY WARREN, 1951

From the time she arrived in Canada, Emily Warren based herself in Ottawa and commuted annually from whatever lodgings she could find there to visit her family's home at 24 Westgate Terrace, Earls Court, London. She would leave Canada each spring to paint the spring flowers and interesting places abroad. She would always have commissions to undertake, and while in England she could calm her apprehensive family.

Eva Gilbert, an Ottawa schoolteacher, made the acquaintance of Bessie Warren and visited the Warren home in the early 1920s. It was a fine old stone mansion of fourteen rooms in an exclusive residential section. She enjoyed the Warrens and described them as 'utterly charming, out of this world entirely'. Mrs Warren 'was a very beautiful woman, more so than any of her daughters. Even at eighty-seven in a wheelchair she was a picture with curly hair, patrician features, and that lovely English tea-rose complexion. She would weep when telling me of the vicissitudes of her baby Emily's life. Emily however, told me that she was a bit tyrannical and favoured "that awful Annie". If you could have seen us going for a picnic to Kensington Gardens, with Chermie's wheelchair piled high with our refreshment, campchairs, easels, wraps, etc. We presented such a picture as Dickens's Pickwickiana. I adored it all.'

During the summers Warren would also renew old friendships, such as that with Mrs Alec Tweedie, wife of a prominent Harley Street physician and a celebrated English author and artist. Ethel Tweedie was famous as a world traveller and during her lifetime published books on her travels to Iceland, Mexico, America, Sicily, Finland and Norway as well as various other books. From 1919 to 1921 she travelled in the East, covering over 50,000 miles, and on her return exhibited 300 water-colours in London. In 1926, she published a book on her experiences, *An Adventurous Journey*. Close friends all their lives, she and Warren shared a love of travel,

A reunion of Mary Warren and daughters in the 1920s.
Front row: Mary Warren and Annie.
Back row: Ada, Bessie, Louie and Emily.

Side Aisle, Westminster Abbey.
c. 1930. 40 x 24 cm.
Description in Warren's hand on the reverse:
'Looking toward the West Door.
Tomb of the Unknown Soldier bearing the inscription
"They buried him among the kings" is at left of the figure.'
Courtesy of Mrs I.A. Kincaid, Toronto.

adventure and art. When Mrs Tweedie died in 1940, she left Warren a small annuity.[1]

Warren would not stay long in London. Much of each summer was spent on the Continent, and she painted in many spots in England. She would often visit one of the cathedral towns to paint the kind of composition in which she gained such distinction. Her ability to contrast flashes of iridescent light amid dark shadows made her cathedral interiors not merely accurate and beautiful, but evocative of the human and spiritual meaning of architecture as Ruskin had taught her to see it.

A large interior of Westminster Abbey showing the Unknown Soldier's grave in the foreground was shown in the British Art Exhibit of 1923. It brought such praise that Queen Mary and Princess Louise requested her to do it in miniature for Queen Mary's Doll's House, which was to be shown to visitors as a means of raising money for the queen's favourite charities and which is still on display at Windsor. Executed on ivory, the miniature painting was only the size of a postage stamp, and only one hair of a brush could be used to do it. Much of the summer was spent sketching on the Continent and doing research for her lectures. She spent more than half of each year, however, in Canada, always returning for the glorious spectacle of autumn. She loved the Gatineau. Each fall she would visit Meach Lake, sketching and painting at Mrs John Hope's cottage. In her old age she had to take the bus from Ottawa and return on the same day.

During her first years in Canada, Warren was able to live in the Ottawa Ladies' College, on First Avenue, where a few professional women were allowed accommodation. Her magnetic presence seemed to unite this group into one happy family. To them she was known as 'Bibbens'; to each member of the group she gave the name of a flower most suited to her personality. Outsiders knew them as 'Wingers' because they occupied the back corridor. Bibbens's room at the extreme end, chosen for its north light, was the furthest from the heating plant, and thus quite uncomfortable, especially on the blustery winter days when, to economize, heat was shut off while everyone else was away at work. In November 1920, the principal of the college, Isobel J. Gallagher, allowed Warren to hold her first Canadian exhibition there. It was a financial success and caused great excitement among those fortunate enough to attend. At about the same time, her large canvasses, draped with flags, were displayed in the windows of Murphy Gamble's store on Sparks Street, one of the major department stores in the capital, to solemnize the Armistice.

---

1. Ethel Brilliana Tweedie, née Harley, was also one of the early noted British women journalists and was active in philanthropic work and in women's causes. She was a Fellow of the Royal Geographical Society.

It was not long after her arrival in Canada that Warren sensed an undertow of jealousy from a few professional people. For that reason she made a public statement to the effect that she would never deprive any Canadian teacher of one penny he might have earned had she not come to Canada. She kept that promise at the cost of great deprivation to herself. In the light of future developments such as the depression and World War II, the wisdom of such a generous offer might be questioned.

Warren supplemented her income during these years by giving lectures, illustrated by lantern slides, in both Canada and Britain. Her method was to have her own paintings photographed, and then from the negatives to have very pale positive impressions made on glass plates. On these, she would meticulously repaint each slide with transparent watercolours, so that each was in fact an exquisite miniature painting. Even with great magnification they still lose nothing of their arresting beauty. These slides can still be seen in the Rare Book Library of the University of Toronto. Former Canadian senator, Eugene Forsey, remembers her both as a fine artist and as a most interesting, excellent lecturer. Her lectures were more than mere travelogues; they were packed with anecdotes and history.

Delivering the lectures across the country required great physical stamina, for each box of slides weighed twelve pounds and was too precious to be entrusted to any porter. Most audiences asked to see a bundle of the actual paintings as well, and often she needed to carry two slide boxes, an umbrella, her own lantern and food for the journey. By the time she included the necessary suitcase of personal belongings, she gave the impression of an itinerant pedlar.

The immediate postwar years were particularly significant for women in England and in North America, and Emily Warren's admiration for pioneers of the women's movement, such as her friends Emmeline Pankhurst in England, Nellie McClung and Judge Emily Murphy of Edmonton, was great. She gave freely to the cause of making the lives of women a little brighter, especially since her experience with male politicians had been so frustrating. It was not an easy task to travel with her equipment to remote villages by train in bleak winter weather, yet she would not refuse an invitation to groups like the Women's Institutes, which were then just organizing.

The Canadian Club was quick to adopt her for lectures to member clubs all over Canada, and churches, schools and colleges followed. Other organizations such as the English Speaking Union, Business and Professional Women's Clubs, women's art associations and university groups were stimulated by her talks. She also lectured in Europe and the United States. Mrs Dean, the wife of Judge Dean of Brookline, Boston, who had been a classmate of Warren at the Royal College of Art, introduced her to audiences there. She spoke at the Boston Public Library, the Brooklyn Institute of Arts and Sciences, New York and the Emma Willard School at Troy, New

York. Columbia University presented her for six successive seasons from 1931 to 1936 as an authority on architecture. In the summer of 1921, as a member of the Ruskin Centenary Council and an authority on John Ruskin, she lectured in Switzerland as part of Sir Henry Lunn's series. Other lecturers included Sir Arthur Conan Doyle and Sir Martin Conway, art critic and mountaineer. That same summer she made an enchanting collection of views of the city of London in all its moods and lights – fog, sunshine, light, shadow, at dawn, at twilight. Her lecture based on these pictures proved very popular since she knew the city so thoroughly and could describe it so well, having been active on the Committee for the Preservation of Old Monuments and having made a thorough study of the city's legends.

Her lectures on Canada were equally popular abroad, and by 1922 she was describing herself to English audiences as a Canadian by adoption. Her first eighteen months in Canada had been a period of intense activity spent finishing the paintings, 'Canada's Tribute', travelling and sketching. Her first lecture on Canada included pictures of historical interest such as the city of Quebec and the Plains of Abraham, as well as views of the Rocky Mountains. At the same time she helped stimulate immigration to Canada by letting her audiences know what the employment opportunities were there. She found such delight living in Canada that she wanted others to share it.

Language was no barrier for Emily Warren, who spoke fluent French. Consultation with Marius Barbeau, ethnologist and folklorist with the National Museum in Ottawa, helped her trace quaint customs and interesting folklore in the province of Quebec. Three of her Quebec sketches were used to illustrate *The Spell of French Canada*, written by her friend Frank Oliver Call, a professor at Bishop's College, Lennoxville, Quebec.[2] The frontispiece to the book was from her painting 'Outdoor Oven, Richelieu Valley'. Another of her illustrations, 'Apple Orchard, Abbey of La Trappe, Oka', depicts the monks, whose order dates back to 1098, labouring in black and white robes among their apple trees in full bloom. A third illustration, 'A Habitant Home of To-day', glows with evening sunlight falling upon a white shrine beside a charming French Canadian farmhouse. The frontispiece to Call's second book in this series, *The Spell of Acadia*, is entitled 'Blomidon in Springtime' and is from one of her paintings. Referring to her only as a friend, not by name, he also quotes her description of the Annapolis Valley orchards. Her words are nearly as evocative as her paintings.

High drifts of snow tinted by the setting sun and blown into cloud-like masses by the sea breeze ... Arches and aisles that run between slender pillars supporting a canopy of unearthly loveliness, a tapestry

2. Frank O. Call, *The Spell of French Canada* (Boston: L.C. Page, 1926).

*beneath arches of light and shadow fit to lead to a palace of an
earthly potentate. And from the hilltop above, looking down over
square miles of blossoms, I felt that here was pure beauty, a beauty
that awes and even hurts. Only once before have I felt the same
and that was one morning in the Alps when I saw for the first time
the clouds in the green valley beneath my feet lighted by the glow
of the rising sun.*[3]

Her extensive travels in Europe were assisted by the railways, which
gave her passes in return for publicity about their various countries.
Similarly, in Canada, the Canadian Pacific and the Canadian National railways gave her passes in return for paintings of views of
her choice. She was especially fond of the mountains, and since these
trips were usually taken in winter they often had their dangerous or
adventurous side. In 1924, she was travelling from Vancouver to
Edmonton on an ill-fated CNR train which met a snow slide. Through
some instinct Warren had not undressed that night and so was
one of the first to trudge through the snow to offer her thermos of
tea to the injured crewmen. In spite of the accident in the mountains,
she reached Edmonton in time for her Canadian Club lecture given
under the auspices of the Edmonton Art and Historical Museum
Association.[4] On one occasion at Lucerne, Alberta, while concen-
trating on the beauty of a scene, she was startled by an oncoming
train and had to leap from a trestle.

On another occasion, she had an adventure with a representative
of the local wildlife: 'That time at Glacier when the train let me off
at two o'clock in the morning, I found the station locked and only a
signal man near the place. I asked him how far it was to the hotel
and he said, "Well, it's quite a ways 'op, ma'am."

' "Is this the road and does it go straight there?" said I.

' "Oh yes, you can't get lost!"

'I then left my bags with instructions to have them sent up next
morning, taking only my sketching things and stool with me. I never
thought of danger and it was just beginning to get light when I heard
what sounded like a human whistle. There was a sort of hedge where
the sound came from, so I walked over and saw the dearest little
fellow about a foot high with a face like a winsome puss, and a very
roguish eye. I said, "Well, I never! Where did you come from, little
brother?" This was where that whistle, which was given me in great
ceremony, on departure for Canada, by a most affectionate and
worried sister Ada, would have been of some use.

3. Frank O. Call, *The Spell of Acadia* (Boston: L.C. Page, 1930), p. 412.

4. One of the special guests on this occasion was Nellie McClung,
suffragette, novelist and a member of the Alberta legislature.

Interior, Anne Hathaway's Cottage.
c. 1930. 28 x 37 cm.
Courtesy of Mrs I.A. Kincaid.

Valley of the Ten Peaks, Lake Louise, Alberta.
c. 1930. 29 x 42 cm.
Courtesy of Mr W. Gammage, London, Ontario.

'Of all things, what on earth shall I do with it? I shall be painting in churches and museums where, if I blew this thing, people would think me crazy. On the only occasion when I could have used it to advantage, I had to substitute a weak human whistle, but we really had a nice conversation that way. Then the little marmot posed for his portrait.'

I believe that this intrepid woman actually enjoyed her reputation of being a 'risky person' regardless of accidents. Had she remained at home as ladies were then expected to do, those people who disapproved, all affluent in comparison, might not have been so harping and derogatory. Because she was so much within public view, however, her business was not entirely her own.

One mysterious project which Warren was working on at this time was a treatise on the Rockies. The portion which I was able to salvage is in the Warren Collection but I do not know if it was published. She experienced the same ecstacy over mountain scenery as did Ruskin, and she shared his ability to convey her vision in words, as this excerpt demonstrates.

Nature seems to have showered on this country every beauty in her generous apron. Imagine if you can a region where the sublimity of the scenery is matched by the beauty, where tremendous peaks lift their foreheads beyond the clouds and black canyons hide their feet in unimaginable depths, where those great leviathans, the glaciers, creep down from the frozen desolation of alpine heights and the black walls of precipices rise up so as to shut out the very light of day, but imagine these softened and balanced by luxuriant pine forests, by smiling green valleys 'murmurous with streams', by the airy veils of silvery waterfalls tumbling against black precipices or green forests and tangling the rainbow in their folds, by the brilliance of alpine uplands sparkling with millions of flowers, and by innumerable magically tinted lakes – imagine these under a sky, 'blue as the sky of fairyland', changing from moment to moment and from hour to hour under varying light and drifting purple cloud shadows, glorified at sunrise and sunset into almost unearthly beauty and transformed by moonlight into a veritable palace of dreams – and you reach some idea of the Canadian Rockies.

One of her favourite spots was Lake Louise, and she left us the following description of her journey to the lake after travelling by train.

From Lake Louise station (5,032 ft.) we take an electric tram on a good carriage road three miles up through the forest to the lake itself, more than 600 feet above. The road runs between tall firs above

*which we catch glimpses of the noble heads of Temple and Lefroy
and as we wind about we have a good view of the Bow valley and
the peaks on its farther side. The air is cool and sweet with balsam
and pine; paint brush and fireweed dot the dark background with
colour; a mad hearted stream leaping from stone to stone, in a wild
rush to the valley, adds the music of tumbling waters. Rounding a
corner we catch our first glimpse of Victoria Glacier and as we pass
through the portico the full glory of the lake bursts upon us.*

Everyone who knew Emily Warren wondered how and why she
continued to shuttle to and fro between Canada and Europe. But she
had several legitimate and even pressing reasons. In the first place
she found less inspiration in Canadian landscape in summer than in
autumn and winter. Next, she had by this time firmly established
her pattern of supporting herself through her lectures and commissioned paintings,[5] as well as by the sale of paintings done at her own
spontaneous decision. Many of her commissions were advance orders
for scenes in the old country, and this as well as the necessity to
prepare new lectures required frequent visits to Europe. Third, she
had family responsibilities that brought her back to England.

Her work was undoubtedly the reason why her trips were annual,
however. 'Art requires travel just as any work has certain requirements,' she once told me, 'but few understand why I keep it up.'

What puzzled the people of Ottawa was her utter disregard of
danger and her cheerfulness. She revealed no sign of the stress which
she was often undergoing. Her letters, however, reveal the haunting
worries of ever increasing responsibilities and declining income as
world depression deepened in the 1930s. She had prepared a lecture
on Ireland which she was to give in Montreal on 15 February 1932,
and she wrote me early that year in the hope that some group in
Toronto would also want it.

*As regards fee, this is a difficult year for so many people and I am
just fitting my fee to their pockets, so please tell them to arrange it
how they like, and how they can afford. I am doing this a good deal
as long as I can get expenses covered; a share of profits is often what
I ask. At one church in Ottawa I had half the takings.*

---

5. Financially, commissions were an important part of her income. Most
were for watercolours, although she could paint equally well in oils. To
give two examples, one request was for a memorial window in a church
in England. It was in honour of an ancestor of the Egerton family of
Ottawa. The other request was from a lady in Temiskaming, Quebec, who
asked Warren to paint the interior of a church in which her great
grandfather had carved the altar.

The summer of 1933 she was again off on her travels and her circuit included Holland, Italy, France, Switzerland, Norway, Sweden, Denmark, and two trips to Spain. This letter from Denmark made Canada's summer heat more bearable.

At Gudvangen July 5 – Quite cool everywhere. I live in coat with sportscoat under and often raincoat too – Very dull, gloomy the last two days but fine scenery. – Many pretty waterfalls.

She was at this time working on a lecture about Scandinavia. Some years later she said in an interview: 'I always seem to have adventures with policemen.' A Danish policeman had been worried about her disregard for the traffic while she tried to find the right spot from which to paint a certain scene. And one time in London on the Thames embankment 'when I hastily threw down my painting paraphernalia that I might get at once to work, a policeman came up hastily, sure that the gesture meant that I was going to throw myself over the railing'.[6]

RMS Caronia
September 14, 1934
As you will see, I am now on my way back for the winter. Am very much afraid it could be a bad season so I feel quite anxious as I now have so many responsibilities at home. Do you think it would be any good to take a room in the Royal York Hotel near the station and have an exhibition there towards the end of November of smallish and other pictures which might sell for Christmas, cathedral interiors as well, of course?

It has been rather a wet summer but I have managed to do a good deal of work. I was in Holland and Belgium and I am finishing preparing a lecture on those two countries.

Also had a week in Ireland at Glengariff – a lovely spot in the south, not a great way from Cork.

Conditions in England are dreadful now as you will have seen by the papers. It will be a great struggle for people to carry on.

Do you think the Queen's Alumnae would care for one of my lectures this season? People seem to like the new one – 'The Charm of England'. I gave it for the first time in New York in March, then for the Overseas League in Paris and then for the Franco-British Alliance in Rouen. I will be back in Ottawa at end of September after a few days in Montreal. This letter never got posted on the boat as I slipped over a step when the boat rocked, caught a door which should have been locked and wasn't, so fell and bruised my right side. Am all strapped up now by the ship's doctor but much better and soon

6. *London Free Press*, 23 April 1940.

will be quite all right. However, I decided to come right back to Ottawa and give up Montreal until October.

I have no letters from her in 1935. The following year during her visit to Europe she was in Spain. Despite shooting in the next block she remained in her hotel in Madrid to finish a painting for her new lecture on that country. When advised to leave, she asked, 'But why? They are not after me.'

About this time began a long silence during which no letters came from Emily Warren, usually a faithful correspondent. I did not understand the reason for it until she gave me a full account years later of what had happened during a sketching visit to Devon with her sister.

We were in Devon at a little cottage where the owner was warming some bedding in front of the fire. I asked for some hot water before going to bed, because the house was very cold. They beckoned to me to help myself from the cauldron on the bracket of the fireplace. I tripped on the blanket, did not know the water was boiling, and a gallon and a half went over my leg.

I really thought then that I would die with the pain. A week later, the local doctor came and peeled all of the skin off without giving me an anaesthetic. The shock was so severe, and the pain so intense, that I could not utter a sound, and went blind. For four months, I could not see. Somehow we got back to London, then to Rosemary, and in two months, my doctor there said, 'Go to Canada; it will be the best cure for you and we can do no more here.'

On shipboard, I was treated just like a leper, but a kind carpenter built me a little shelf so that I did not have to crawl about on the floor. No one tried to help me, and my trays were just thrown down as for an animal.

I landed in New York on February 28 [1937].

The sleeper to Montreal carried a victorious and very noisy hockey team, who spent the whole night carousing. One of them, however, sensing my illness, stood guard beside my berth most of the night.

Finally, I arrived at Maycourt [a boarding house], Ottawa. Not realizing that I could not stand alone, they let me crawl upstairs to bed. My dear friend, Dr William Stevens, visited me next morning and I told him of an engagement to lecture at Columbia University two weeks hence. He said, 'You have come all this way alone. I see no reason why you cannot go to New York.' Promising to do everything he suggested, I waited in suspense, using any moment when I felt well enough to colour some of the lantern slides to be used. There was some surprise in that house when I told them my plans, but I gave the lecture speaking from a chair. No lame person should ever be expected to stand very long.

After this extremely serious injury, her leg was never entirely as it had been, and in later years it pained and incapacitated her more and more. As Emily Warren aged, its effects joined with those of other injuries she received in her energetic travels, and with the influenza and bronchitis that afflicted her chronically. Her increasing physical difficulties, however, could never long depress her, diminish her enthusiasm for painting and people, or break her intense will to be active and independent.

After the interval occasioned by the injury to her leg, her correspondence continued as before.

From the Cunard Liner, Ascania
September 14, 1937
I expect this will seem like a breath from the past; it is so long since
I have seen you. I am getting back to normal again after over a
year's hindrance and serious illness with my scalded foot and leg.
Of course the money loss has been dreadful and I will have to work
very hard to make up for it and pay my debts. Am much hoping that
I may be able to get a lecture or two in Toronto.

October 4, 1937
Am going to stay with Mrs Crate at Mary Lake, Muskoka for a little
from October 10th.[7]
There is a kind of vague chance that the Toronto Canadian Club
might like a lecture. Yes, the Spanish lecture was finished in March
last and I have given it at Brooklyn, New York, also at Montreal and
here too. People seem to like it. Of course, I have no war horrors in
it. Isn't it terrible the awful things that have been done?

November 27, 1938
Seems ages since I've seen you. Never went further than Montreal
last time I was in Canada. Have been very busy painting Royal
Gardens. Did a view of the little summer house with masses of roses
and plants in front of it. The queen is very fond of it.
From Emmie, King's Lynn, England

The following year, despite the increasing certainty of another world war, Warren again travelled to the Continent. In fact she left Italy for England only after frantic pleas from family and friends. She was there when war broke out.

---

7. Mrs John Crate was the wife of the editor of the Ottawa *Journal.* Although it was Emily's custom to spend Christmas with the Hope family, New Year's Eve was reserved for party fun at the home of Mr and Mrs John Crate. As master of ceremonies Warren made these occasions very memorable for the circle of friends who attended.

St. Mary's Cottage. Whitstone,
Holsworthy. North Devon.
November 29, 1939

As you will see, I did not get over in September. My sisters were too anxious and nervous about the air raids etc. We let our Surrey house and took this most primitive cottage unfurnished, just picnicing here with a little furniture sent from 'Rosemary'. It is a most remote place 225 miles from London, a few scattered cottages, a church, a chapel and a shop. I feel rather like a prison inmate for it has poured steadily for six weeks. However, as it is such a safe place, I feel I can leave my sisters and have decided to come to Canada in early January. They are now quite content for me to do that and it is highly necessary as my big pictures are now stored in a damp, dark place and they will deteriorate if left, especially as I still have more to do to them after their spoiling at McGill College.

Alas, I must try and make a little of the needful to keep the 'Home Fires' burning, so much more is needed now that my sisters have aged so much.

Do you think there are any churches or other societies which might like a lecture? I am putting in my list of subjects. People seemed to like the Scandinavian one, but there are several new ones which I have not given in Toronto.

So stoney broke this year, I am sending no Christmas presents or cards even.

It was not long, however, before she arrived back in Canada on urgent business.

CHAPTER IV

The Darkening Perspective

*If we fill our brain with beautiful thoughts, there can be
no room for evil ones.*
EMILY WARREN, 1952

Not long after World War II had broken out, a letter from a friend in
Montreal had warned Warren that the big pictures, then at McGill
University, were in jeopardy; the colours 'had faded'. Actually, the
colours had blackened. She had been asked by Dean Ira Mackay to
permit the paintings to be hung in McGill's Moyse Hall, an appropriate place because Sir Arthur Currie, one of the central figures,
was then the principal. However, they were placed over radiators
which, when the steam was turned on, caused the lower third of the
paintings to darken. As soon as passage was available, therefore, she
risked a wartime crossing to come to their rescue. I heard from her
early in the new year.

Ottawa, January 26, 1940
*Directly I have done what I can to the big pictures and got them
varnished, I must go back to my sisters. Dreadful things may happen
any time or they may even happen before I can get back. Hitler
and his Nazis are to my mind like the devil and his angels!*

*However, my sisters are in the safest place they could be in, so
far away in the west and such a tiny place. It was a very rough sea
passage. Fortunately for me I have never been seasick but nearly all
the other passengers were ill. There were 70 only in the tourist
class where I was one of ten English. The others were Germans,
Austrians, Jews, etc., poor things, all so glad to get away. Such
dreadful things they told me – the unspeakable doings of Hitler's
Huns.*

*We had to take our lifebelts wherever we went on the ship and
it was a blackout, all windows, portholes, etc. painted black and thick
wooden shutters clamped over them. It made it rather depressing,
especially as, being so rough, it was impossible to go on deck. At
4:00 p.m. the blackout bugle sounded. No one went out except the
policemen to patrol the deck and watch. We had life boat drill and
one alarm drill when we were in the most dangerous part. There was*

no convoy but ours was a quick ship (it took eleven days, though, from Liverpool to New York) ...

General MacBrien arranged space for her in the Justice Building in Ottawa where it took her eight months to repaint the faces. Though they were still not finished to her satisfaction, space there had to make way for a war department, so they were moved to the Bank of Montreal, where they hung from September 1940 to January 1941. At the request of Prime Minister Mackenzie King, they were then transferred to the main entrance hall of the Centre Block of the Parliament Buildings leading to the entrance of the Library of Parliament, where, under proper lighting, the public could once more enjoy them. Of course, she bore all expenses herself. Insurance costs amounted to $50.00 per year and transfer charges had to be paid out of her own pocket.

Warren's most pressing concerns through the war were helping her three remaining sisters in England (by then elderly and in failing health) and earning a living. Her annuity from Mrs Tweedie was suspended by the public trustee for the duration of the war. And her lectures, which had provided her with a steady source of income, were less in demand as everyone's energies and thoughts were increasingly focussed on the war.

Ottawa, March 11, 1940
... As regards the lectures, I have just heard that I am to lecture at Whitby Ladies' College, April 12th and at Port Hope April 19th. In the interim, I go to Hamilton and paint a picture of the interior of the basilica. Mr [Hugh] Cunningham of the Art Gallery [National Gallery] advised me to do this a couple of years ago as he felt sure it would sell, so I am going to chance it, though it is very difficult to squeeze in the time.

Ottawa, March 18, 1940
There is much grippe here. I have been fighting germs a good deal – not incapacitated but it is everywhere I go and I must keep up the warfare. It's too expensive to be ill. Have been wondering whether you would care for me to bring any slides and give you and any of your friends a little show? Shall have the Scandinavian slides anyway as I am giving that at Whitby. You haven't seen those for it is my newest.

Friends who had previously enjoyed her informal talks were happy to forget about war for an evening and journey with her through Denmark, Sweden and Norway. Towards the end of the lecture she demonstrated how, by sitting up all night on a coastal steamer, she had sketched the magnificent kaleidoscope of the midnight sun.

Henry VII Chapel, Westminster Abbey.
1916. 71 x 51 cm.
Similar to the view commissioned by Queen Mary for the twenty-first
birthday of Edward, Prince of Wales. It was Warren's opinion that
the chapel contains Europe's finest example of fan tracery vaulting.
Private collection.

A Garden, Ottawa South.
c. 1940. 31 x 21½ cm.
Courtesy of General R.T. Bennett, Ottawa.

Now, because of the war she was unable to get transportation back to Britain. However, she spent time doing illustrations and painting watercolours and oils of outstanding Canadian landscapes including 'Apple Blossoms, Wolfville, Nova Scotia' and 'Valley of the Ten Peaks' commissioned for the Canadian Pacific Railway and 'Columbia Ice Field', 'Mount Robson, the Rockies' and 'Cape Smokey, Cape Breton' commissioned for the Canadian National Railway.

She was very worried about her sisters. With communications disrupted by the war she often was without news. Late in 1940 she wrote me that she had heard nothing for a month. She had sent a reply cable for Christmas. In the spring I heard further.

Ottawa, April 21, 1941

It seems suddenly to have burst into summer here – so warm and the trees are budding so fast. It has been for me, as well as for so many others, a very anxious time. All of my sisters have been dangerously ill in England. I nearly went back but the three sisters are now slowly recovering and have kept on cabling for me not to come. Also the doctor wrote me a long letter saying 'don't come'. Fortunately, they now have two very capable women looking after them. Ada has not yet recovered from the neuritis in her stomach.[1] Louie, who has arthritis in her knees, fell and broke her leg (it is mended now). Bessie tried to lift her and got strangulated hernia and other internal troubles and for six weeks her life was despaired of. You can imagine what an awful time it has been. I was constantly sending reply-paid cables.

Do you know anyone who has a pretty garden who might like a picture of it? I did some for people here last year and they were very pleased. Have also just been painting the interior of a friend's room. These make quite pretty little pictures done small. I could send a specimen to show anyone.

Alas, I fear the Hamilton Basilica Interior is not getting sold. Mr Cunningham had it framed and I've got to pay $10.50 for the frame and the express charges here. Wilson's Gallery is being closed and my last exhibition there will begin April 28th. Of course nothing matters but the war, though one has to live. All this about my own tiresome affairs. Too bad to bother you. Have had a horrid time with grippe and anemia – now rheumatism or something in right arm, but it will all pass.

My offer of a short trip for a spring tonic was turned down.

Ottawa, May 13

It would have been lovely if I could have seen the apple blossoms

----

1. Ada died in September 1941.

*at Niagara but I hear that is to be the time for me at Manotick. Shall,
of course, be selling my work there so must not miss it.*

Special commissions interrupted her tight schedule.

Ottawa, May 22
*Have been taken up doing another wedding present but will be able
to get on now. Apple blossoms not out yet at Manotick so it may be
right into June before I can come in to Toronto.*

*Have to help the Red Cross, fortune telling, on May 27th, also
June 2nd at a garden party, so that will hold me back too! The
mosquitos are beginning also! Three in this house caught yesterday.
They always go for me so I really cannot go in places where they
abound.*

*There is a little idea on now about my doing something for CNR –
not out West though, alas, but I won't be able to stay very long.*

That spring she was busy painting the apple blossoms at Manotick,
and then went to Quebec, to the Île d'Orléans, to sketch and to gather
anecdotes for her talks about Canada abroad. The CNR was giving
her a pass and in return she was to paint them an oil painting. She
also did some fortune telling that spring which she did frequently at
garden parties during the war to raise money for the Red Cross. Her
psychic predictions and her ability to weave a story made her fortunes
good entertainment.

As the war continued her spirits seemed to flag somewhat. She
suffered from the flu and had difficulty finding accommodation that
suited her. I wrote her an encouraging letter late in 1942 and
received the following reply.

December 4, 1942
*Thank you so much for all you have done and are doing for me; I
do indeed appreciate it – though I am so slow in acknowledging it.
Have really no hopes or expectations of any of my plans and ideas
materializing.*

*Really, nothing but the war matters, though I had thought that
perhaps the old cathedrals which the boys are fighting to preserve
might have been interesting, and English things too. Have been down
with the grippe. Now have laryngitis but it isn't enough to prevent
my keeping on.*

*My landlady has been awful. Isn't it a mercy we have the rent
control people? It wasn't a question of rent at all, except she wanted
to turn me out and put two or three girls in my room. However, the
lawyer has told her that she can't turn me out without some reasons.*

*Have just had my little Autumn Exhibition. Sold quite a few small
pictures I am glad to say. Never mind if things don't turn out well*

Emily Warren restoring damage to the 'Canada's Tribute' paintings
in the Justice Building, Ottawa, 1939.
Photograph by Elsa Herwig for the Ottawa *Citizen*.

'Our Little Greenhouse', Hampton, Ontario.
c. 1940. 22 x 15 cm.
Courtesy of Mrs Leonard Monkman, Toronto.

*for me – they rarely do. Out of fifty endeavours, one, perhaps not
that, succeeds. It has been so all my life.*

*Have been busy in a way but, of course, illness puts one back and
the days now are so dark for painting.*

In January she visited me in Toronto as she had been giving lectures
in Port Hope and Whitby. She then went to visit her cousin at
Lennoxville, Quebec, the Reverend Frank Vial, at that time emeritus
professor of pastoral theology and an invalid. But these were the last
lectures she gave to schools during the war. Her friends did their
best to help out, but because everyone's energies were devoted to the
war, all efforts to appeal on her behalf to Toronto schools, churches,
individuals, in fact anyone who knew her, were without avail at that
time. Her bad leg, too, was bothering her and she was not well enough
to paint for much of the summer of 1943.

Late that year she received a cable that her sister Bessie was dying,
and she began to make arrangements to return to England as quickly
as possible. Her other sister Louie, although in good general health,
was helpless from arthritis and had to be lifted from her chair to bed.
Before she was able to arrange passage, however, Bessie died, and
urgent business at home persuaded her to put off her return for a
time. Friends were trying to make arrangements about her big
pictures and she desperately wanted to have them settled before she
left. On 31 March 1944 she wrote: 'Am hoping to get over to England
just as soon as the picture matter is settled "yes" or "no". I expect the
latter ...' In fact she discovered that Cunard was not booking pas-
sages and had a long waiting list. She hoped to get passage in June
or July.

> . *Ottawa, May 29, 1944*
> *... Life is a difficult matter ... Louie is so wanting me back in England.*
> *Mrs Bodin (the housekeeper) I am almost thankful to say will not*
> *come back to Rosemary with us and that's a great relief after what*
> *I've heard about her, so I am hoping to get passage the end of June*
> *or early July. No return tickets issued and I've been warned it will be*
> *a long time before I can return so at present my plan is if all is well*
> *and I can get Louie comfortably fixed at Rosemary with a kind,*
> *competent housekeeper – not nurse really – but just able to lift her*
> *with help, all will be well. I will let top of the house – four nice rooms*
> *and bath, and be with Louie downstairs.*
>
> *September 1946, will hope to return here for Autumn colours,*
> *exhibition and lectures, and then pack up and take over my posses-*
> *sions. Don't know how I'll keep things going, but will do somehow.*
> *Suppose you won't be coming to Ottawa at all? I've so much to do,*
> *commissions for little pictures, etc. which must be done, or I can't*
> *pay all I have to.*

Once again her departure was delayed.

August 4, 1944
As you will see, I have not gone yet. There are many complications
and difficulties and I feel dreadfully worried. The people won't, and
I suppose also can't leave our house on account of [the shortage of]
accommodation. Isn't it a predicament? A friend of mine in England
is trying all in her power and I am writing to likely places, also to
ask friends if they know any nursing homes. England, I hear, is in a
state of chaos and conditions are very difficult in every way. Also
perhaps Louie won't go to a nursing home even if we find one, so I
am just living from day to day.

Finally she decided that she would need to remain in Canada for the
time being. They were not able to get their house, Rosemary, back
while the war was going on, and it was necessary that Warren help
financially which she could not easily do in England. Bessie's pension,
the larger, ceased at her death, and Louie did not have enough to
live on. Warren had been sending £100 per year in better times. She
could not now afford to send that but she had managed to send about
£75. 'If I go over, it will take pretty well that amount for getting over
only and when there I have no means whatever of earning anything.
Yet, it does on the one hand seem so cruel (it will to her, I know) if I
cannot get over – on the other hand, we could not live without money
and have no relatives to help.'
    In March 1946 she wrote to me from England.

St. Mary's, Whitstone,
Holsworthy, England
I had a cable 'come quickly'. Rushed here by plane from Montreal to
Prestwick in Scotland in 12 hours, 45 minutes. Then plane to
London and train here.
    Arrived last Friday. My sister could speak then and was so glad
to see me as she sat in her chair, but the rheumatoid arthritis
attacked her heart and the result of the two accidents took their toll.
Louie died on Sunday and the funeral was yesterday. Am cleaning
out cottage and selling furniture, but greater part is demanded by
those awful women who came in to clean and the housekeeper
demands all she can of my possessions! However, I leave here on
Friday next for London for a week to arrange all sorts of business ...
    This is indeed a hectic time for me. Will be returning to Canada
in September.

That summer she was detained in England over estate matters but
was able to get around a good deal to fulfil commitments and also to
paint several other 'English bits', including two beautiful pictures of

Lion's Head Inn, Thursley, Surrey.
c. 1941. 17 x 19 cm.
This old pub was near the rehabilitation camp for Canadians
supervised by the Lorne Scots of Brampton, Ontario, during World War II.
Private collection.

The Old Curiosity Shop, London.
c. 1946. 17 x 18 cm.
Each Warren interpretation of this often commissioned subject
included Little Nell and her grandfather.
Courtesy of Mrs Marion Taylor, Toronto.

Westminster Parliament Buildings at sunset (one is now in the possession of former Senator Eugene Forsey). She was at that time seventy-seven years old.

London, June 25, 1946
I am moving about a good deal as there is much to arrange and see about, I being now the last of my family. Have also several commissions to execute and will be going up to Scotland for a while later on. I must see about the Rosemary house and mean to sell the furniture when I get the tenants out. It is in the hands of two agents now ...

Warren returned to Ottawa in the fall, by airplane. As one might expect in such an intrepid traveller, who had made 38 crossings by sea, she took to air transport without a care for any danger. The smaller the plane the better she liked it.

101 James Street, Ottawa
October 12, 1946
I flew over from England last Sunday, a perfect day and wonderful flight. It was impossible to get a passage for about two years. Have sold the house and furniture – not very well but I am glad it is all over. Had a very strenuous time in the doing of it. Poor old England is in an awful state of chaos. The destruction was shocking. Have to give a lecture at Hamilton a little later for the Business and Professional Women's Club. Do wish I could get one in Toronto too, for I am only to be allowed to bring very little money from England and not yet. At the moment, I am up at Meach Lake. Autumn colours going fast. It is pouring in buckets so I am writing a few letters.

November 23, 1946
Am starting a little Exhibition today at the Children's Library on Laurier Avenue ... Yes, I have quite a few English bits. Had to be in England several months before the evacuee people could be got out, so I moved about a bit and painted, staying as long as I could keep a roof over my head. There are quite a few cottages and gardens and will send some for you to choose from when the show is over. Did several bits in London where, at the Girls' Friendly Society Lodge, it was more possible to be able to stay. Have two of the Westminster Parliament Buildings at sunset. Am afraid Hamilton is 'off'. I wrote to them, i.e. the Business and Professional Women's Club, from England and directly I got back, but have heard nothing. However, now the war is over, perhaps people will like ordinary things more. Will see if the Port Hope people would like a lecture and Whitby College also, but that would be after Christmas. Am going over to England next year – cannot get all the business arranged – family

portraits, etc. to see after, and the graves – they are really nothing but I must keep the memorial and the cross and steps are not even begun yet. Also I cannot get a cent of the sale money for either house or furniture. The lawyer is investing it in England. I can spend it when I get over there only. There is a good deal more to do, so it is my only choice.

It was a year earlier that the Ottawa *Citizen* had stated: 'Miss Warren can be looked upon as as much of a Canadian as a native English-woman by virtue of her long sojourns in this country over many years.'[2] In spite of all difficulties, her love for Canada remained. In 1929 and 1939 Canadian passports had been issued in her name. Her dual status was confirmed by the Canada Citizenship Act of 1 January 1947 which stated that all former British subjects living in Canada at that time who arrived before 1942 automatically became Canadian citizens.

Afterward she fulfilled the requirements for the old age pension, and was able to use that toward nursing care at the very end of her life. This regular monthly income, even though small, could not have come at a more opportune time. The years of World War II left her bereft of family. She had suffered bitter disappointment over the serious damage to her most prized work. Her money from the sale of the house in England could not be brought to Canada. Expected lectures were cancelled. She was too ill to paint during one of her few summers spent in Canada yet her ambition and ability to do so remained as strong as ever.

---

2. Ottawa *Citizen*, 17 November 1945.

CHAPTER V

The Most Faithful
Devotee of Art

*Fine Art is that in which hand and head and heart
have worked equally together.*
JOHN RUSKIN to Emily Warren
Circa 1885

During her absence in England, Warren's friends had continued to
work for the sale of her important historical paintings.[1] On 12 August
1946, Russell Boucher, Progressive Conservative member for Carle-
ton, raised the question of the paintings, 'Canada's Tribute', in the
House of Commons, stating that he believed they could be acquired
at reasonable cost. 'I feel,' he said, 'that if the pictures are worthy of
hanging in the main hall of this building for such a long time, on
loan, it ill befits the government to continue their use without purchasing them. I would argue that the lady be approached and the
pictures purchased by the government.'[2] In reply the minister of
public works explained that the government itself makes no purchase
of paintings, but votes funds for the acquisition of paintings, those
funds being administered by the board of the National Gallery.
Boucher then suggested that the board of the gallery be asked to
purchase the paintings.

Whether or not this intervention in the House had any effect, the
paintings were in fact finally sold late in 1947. The letter Warren
wrote to her good friend Ottilie Herwig in London, whom she had
seen while abroad that summer, has survived.

January 10, 1948

Dear Ottilie:
    *I too had a very nice Christmas as usual with the Hopes. At
present I am having a nice restful week-end with a friend in Montreal ... Thank goodness the business is finally settled about the big
pictures, thanks to my wonderful friends. It will remain a miracle
how they achieved it. I only got half the sum I asked – just enough
to pay for the materials and some of the travelling, i.e. $5,000.00*

1. See Appendix B.

2. Canada, House of Commons, *Debates*, 1946, V, 4670.

but, the great point is that all is settled and some of the money is invested. So when my old age comes, I will be able to live without being a burden to anyone – there is really no one I could be a burden to. It is a great relief and I am indeed grateful to the many people who helped in so many ways. 'Let the dead past bury its dead.' The pictures are now in the Sir Arthur Currie Memorial Hall at the Military College, Kingston.

Although I had a number of letters from her during that winter, spring and summer, I did not hear of the sale until I received the following along with other news in a letter dated 27 September 1948, Ottawa.

Life was quite strenuous and difficult in England this year and I fear I did not write as many letters as I should. Am now only just settled down at the same place as last year. So glad to be here with bright light and with such nice people. You will be surprised to hear of the miracle which has occurred to me. My wonderful friends have somehow worked very hard at the awful tangle. The government is going to buy the two big pictures, but only for half the original price. Still $5,000.00 will pay for me at an old ladies' home when I get doddery. Am indeed thankful to have that load of worry lifted, for the pictures are so large.

She did not mention to me anything of the disposition of the proceeds. She knew that in my concern for her welfare I would have asked what had happened to the part of the money which was not invested. Seven years later she told me of her own accord (and her diary confirms the fact) that the remainder had been borrowed within a week of her receiving it by someone she considered a close friend – she was then seventy-eight years old. It was on this occasion that her faith in her fellow human beings suffered a most severe blow: the loan was never repaid.

The amazing thing about Warren was her ability to overcome the effects of such setbacks and to continue working. Tension, over-exertion and malnutrition contributed to her frequent illnesses. One day I found her walking to a distant location for a day's sketching with but a handful of biscuits for nourishment. My concern at the time must have registered because there are frequent references to her diet in subsequent letters.

One of her great concerns in 1947 and 1948 was what was to become of John Ruskin's home in the Lake District, Brantwood. It had been given to Oxford University, and Warren had been shocked to learn from the vice chancellor in the summer of 1947 that it was to be made into a hostel. 'Isn't it abominable?' she wrote. 'The house should be kept as a shrine like the Longfellow house in USA, the

Brantwood on Coniston Water, England.
c. 1911. The frontispiece for *Homes and Haunts of John Ruskin*.
The original (21½ x 29 cm) is in the Ruskin Galleries,
Bembridge School, Isle of Wight, UK.

Friar's Crag.
c. 1911. Where Ruskin's early appreciation of nature was aroused.
From *Homes and Haunts of John Ruskin*.

Emerson house, etc.' She then undertook a vigorous campaign, writing to college and university presidents and principals to urge them to support Brantwood's preservation. She travelled to Boston to speak to the Ruskin Club and while there enlisted the help of a number of prominent people. In September 1948 she let me know the results of her efforts.

About Brantwood, there is good news too. Mr [J.H.] Whitehouse who gave it to Oxford University, has now taken it back so now in Perpetuity, it will belong, I trust, to the world, USA and Britain and probably others, for there will be a need of a good deal of financing. Anyway, it won't be made into a Hostel.

When I learned of the sale of the 'Canada's Tribute' paintings and thus the change in her affairs, the time seemed opportune to suggest a holiday. Thirty years previously we had vowed to go together some day to the Rocky Mountains. I had spent a year there just before she arrived in Canada, and had always been fond of the scenery; but when she began to illuminate it with her technique, it was transformed for me. We were not able, however, to arrange it that year. In fact it was not until 1951 that we managed a holiday together.

Early in 1949 she wrote me that she would be flying to England on 6 April. Voyages by sea she now found too uncomfortable and it cost only about $40.00 more to fly. When I told her that I was planning a trip to Europe that summer she suggested an itinerary. The following letter provides a glimpse at how she lived in these years during her travels.

Ottawa, March 8, 1949
I am delighted that you are coming to England. We must certainly meet. I shall be in London for a week from April 5th. Then I go to Switzerland for a few days en route to the Riviera where I have a commission to paint a couple of little pictures. I can only be away about three and a half weeks in all, except a week in France. It is so expensive in Italy for accommodation, but France at Chartres has the finest stained glass in Europe. In London you could stay at the same place that I do – the Girls' Friendly Diocesan Lodge, 29 Francis Street, Westminster, close to Victoria Station, the Abbey, etc. There are always from 60 to 75 girls and ladies of the professional classes staying there. The fees are $15.00 per week for a nice little bedroom, breakfast, porridge, two pieces of toast or bread and butter, tea or coffee, generally a very small piece of bacon and potatoes or fish. No lunches served as everyone is out, but at 7:15 p.m. there is dinner, soup, fish, or very small portion of meat and potatoes and cabbage – generally two desserts, jam tart or prunes. There is always hot water, day or night, a nice library and lounge and all the daily papers, but

people must be recommended, so if you think of going, mention my
name for they know me very well. In June I will be at Stratford,
about the first week. Do ask me anything you like for I know quite
a few places you would like.

She was in Port Hope later that month to give a lecture at Trinity
College, and then came to Toronto to visit and gave a little talk for
several friends. True to her word she offered suggestions for our
journey. Unfortunately she went back to Ottawa with a bad cold.

One of her reasons for settling in Canada had been to avoid
bronchitis which plagued so much of her life in England, and she
was very susceptible to colds and flu. But no mere cold or flu could
keep her in one place. Now in her eightieth year, beset with all sorts
of financial difficulties and infirmities, she flew to London before the
end of March. Day after day her diary revealed that she felt 'queer'
as the flu ran its course. Of necessity, she had to leave her bed to
obtain ration books, passport, tickets from Cook's and to see a doctor.
However, a fortnight later she flew to Paris, and then continued on
by a tedious train trip of twenty-four hours for Switzerland. Quite
exhausted, she reached Spiez Wednesday, 13 April, before ten o'clock
in the morning.

The warm sunshine felt so wonderful that she went to Oberhofen
in the afternoon, lining up possibilities for sketching. Two days later
she wrote in her diary about drawing from the boat on the Lake of
Thun and painting the castle, a favourite subject with the glistening
Bernese Oberland mountains for a background. Then the weather
changed and became uncomfortably warm. Warren was a devout
Anglican but she attended the Lutheran Church on Sunday morning.
After church she completed her drawings and packed in preparation
to move on. Although far from well, she could still glory in the
familiar Swiss scenes – 'the glaring mountains, wonderful!' She arrived at Zermatt and next afternoon sketched the Matterhorn. At
5:45 a.m. the following morning she completed the sketch by filling
in the sunrise colours on the peak. Three hours later she was on the
train for S. Margherita, a trip which took the full day; the train was
crowded and she had to stand during most of the journey. It was no
wonder, therefore, that her knee gave trouble later.

Stopping at Portofino, San Remo, Menton, she managed to do at
least one sketch every day. Then, when Sunday came around again
she rested. Monday brought rain but that did not prevent her sketching from a lighthouse – 'gales of wind swept some of my papers into
the sea'. By mid-afternoon she was bound for Cannes but stayed over
at Grasse. It rained there; consequently she could only do a 'scramble
bit' in a doorway. Thence she went to Antibes, which she found all
changed; she sketched its flower market. Next day, by bus, she
reached Nice and was very disappointed: 'The market was ugly and

The Bow River in Moonlight.
Date unknown. Oil on canvas. 51 x 81 cm.
Courtesy of Mrs Shirley Johannsen, Old Chelsea, Quebec.

The Jungfrau from the Castle of Manfred.
From *Homes and Haunts of John Ruskin.*

the flowers all wrapped in paper!' By Sunday she was in Chartres, the site of her favourite cathedral because 'it has the finest stained glass in the world'. Dull weather closed in making it too dark to paint, cold and depressing. However, she managed to get one sketch of a little old street, Rue Yves.

Had it not been for her diary, I should have had no conception of the pace she maintained. It would take several pages to describe the other places which she visited that summer; suffice it to say that there were seventy-seven trips by train or bus, seventeen visits to former friends, and an output of at least sixty-six sketches.

The diary also reveals the depth of her dedication. Weather affected her so much that conditions were recorded almost every day along with the effect upon her. Late in the summer she wrote to me.

London, August 7, 1949
I shall be at the GFS until Saturday when I leave very early in the morning to go to friends at Milford-on-Sea. Could we meet on the 11th or 12th? Shall not be back here again until September 5th to 12th when I leave for Canada.

Realizing how precious time was to her, I met her just long enough to report my and my companions' travels thus far, especially the trip which she had suggested through Switzerland, the Italian lakes and the French Riviera. She must have notified the proprietors of the hotels in advance and was much amused to hear about our rumpled appearance when we approached the Inn on the Park at Lake of Lugano on foot. We had failed to notice a car which was sent to the railway station to meet us.

The winter of 1949-50 in Canada was rather a difficult one for Emily Warren. She first had trouble finding accommodation. She took rooms on a temporary basis while she tried to find first an apartment, and then just a room that fitted her requirements of the proper light, heat and a pleasant (and tolerant) landlady. She also had her difficulties executing her commissions. She was painting an autumn scene of McGregor Lake in the Gatineau that fall for Charlotte Whitton (at that time a controller on the city council and later a mayor of Ottawa) to be presented by a chapter of the Imperial Order of the Daughters of the Empire to St. Hilda's residence, Trinity College, University of Toronto, in memory of Margaret Grier, a former student. She was having some trouble and she wrote me of her difficulties.

I had such a problem to get up the Gatineau. It finally ended in my being driven up. Morning light was the right one but we didn't arrive until after noon and had lunch first. That day was practically lost for we had to return at 3:30 p.m. I decided it would have to be an

oil; next day just got one and a half hours quick sketching in the
morning as there was nowhere to stop – it meant driving two hours
there and two back. It's horribly difficult ... but, of course, I must
do my best.

Still her spirits never flagged for long. In the same letter she wrote:
'Have a wild plan to paint some of the mountains in the Rockies in
snow, but can't afford to do that unless I can get a few lectures en
route ... I want to have an exhibition of cathedrals and mountains[3] in
1951.' She decided in the end not to go west that winter. She visited
me in February, and gave several lectures with slides to small groups,
then went on to Niagara Falls to visit friends and give further talks.
Unfortunately she again succumbed to flu and did not shake it off.
For the first time she felt unable to manage and wrote me of her
worries on 7 March.

My landlady is – !!! Words fail.
    Because I have got virus flu, no nursing home will take me and
the hospitals are so overcrowded. The doctor said when I had said,
'I don't want to go to hospital', 'I certainly don't blame you', so I am
doing everything for myself as I have always had my own little grill,
eating fruit and taking eggs and milk and now some Bovril too but
I feel far from well.

Two weeks later she wrote again.

This horrible flu has pulled me down again and I can't seem to
shake it off, especially the depression which always results. I get
waves of feeling better, then in a short time the horrible feeling as
if one were going to die, comes on. There is nothing to do, the doctor
says, but lie down. When I get a brief space of feeling better, I do
things and in the end, I will be well I know. Have already booked a
berth in a boat for England the middle of March, 1951 for I can
never afford to go by air again.

This last comment indicates how firmly the depression had taken
hold, because by this time she was an inveterate flyer. Of course by
the following year she had long since bounced back and cancelled
the berth on the ship in order to go by air. That year she visited
cousins in Newfoundland both on her way to and from England.[4]

---

3. She had planned to call this exhibition 'The Cathedrals of Man and of
Nature.'

4. On 11 August 1950 the St. John's *News* devoted a long article to
Warren and her work on the occasion of her impending visit.

Chartres Cathedral, the South Ambulatory.
Date unknown. 46 x 32 cm.
Private collection.

Meach Lake, Quebec.
c. 1924. Oil on canvas. 47½ x 70 cm.
Courtesy of Mrs Hugh MacMillan.

There were Warren and Bowring cousins there, the best known of whom was Eric Bowring, CBE, chairman of the board of Bowring's. Eric Bowring had planned to publish a history of the firm with some illustrations by Emily Warren.[5] He also suggested that she paint the interior of the St. John's Cathedral. She started work on it that year, but her first attempts were ruined by poor materials purchased locally. So she returned to St. John's in August of 1951 to do the cathedral picture for her cousin.

In 1950, we again began to talk about our trip together; this time we thought of including a visit to Carmel, California. Emily Warren had always been curious to learn more about the chain of missions built by Spanish monks along the coast of California at a distance from each other of one day's walk. A cousin travelling to England from New Zealand had singled out one in particular in Carmel, a very picturesque place, first settled by a group of German artists. American tourists in Switzerland also told Emily of the lovely scenery at Carmel. She wrote to me of her plans at a time when the Korean crisis was dominating everyone's mind.

January 27, 1951
I really do not know what to say in face of all the circumstances. If war comes, I think I shall have to rush over to England first and do as many commissions as possible before I go out West. Expect I could go West even if there is a war ... Am afraid I seem very useless about the travel, really don't know what to do but in a few days, we'll probably hear definitely about the war. Of course it would be very beautiful in California but my time is really almost planned – April out West, May at Kew Gardens, Shottery, etc. and June 7th to Northumberland, which was fixed last year. Have quite a few commissions for Hathaway place and also Kew Gardens.[6]

Am going in a day or so to enquire about various mountains and see CNR people. I have to do a large picture in oil, 40 × 30, from whatever mountain view they choose. This is to pay for transportation and, of course, is done here in the Autumn from which sketch they like best. Am bound to finish the interior of St. John's cathedral, Newfoundland, which I've just begun. If I go to England, it is a question of income and getting pictures for my exhibition, commissions, etc. of which I have a good many.

---

5. The book was published without her illustrations six years after her death. David Keir, *The Bowring Story* (London, 1962).

6. She regularly visited Lord and Lady Armstrong, at Cragside, Rothbury, Northumberland; she painted the gardens which were especially noted for their rhododendrons. Her interiors of Anne Hathaway's cottage were much in demand and were one of her most important commission scenes for earning her livelihood.

Am hoping (if only the days would get lighter) to finish the interior by early March but it is a large oil and I have other things to work on too. Am so sorry to be so undecided. If war comes, that will settle it one way or another.

Of course I'd love to see California. Was going once to stay with friends there but life and time seem so short now. Have sent you a jumble but it will let you see that I've started thinking and planning.

Eventually our arrangements were made. Starting out separately, we converged at Monterey, and although she was then eighty-two years old, there was no doubt whatever that she would keep the tryst. As she stepped off the train from San Francisco, I marvelled at her smart appearance (in a neatly tailored dark green suit with felt hat to match) and her light-hearted manner.[7] 'What magnificent pine trees; where do these come from?' she remarked as the taxi pulled away from the station in the half light of evening. I explained that they were a rapid-growing variety of pine imported from Australia.

After a two-mile drive through high wooded country, Carmel, with its tidy little homes and gardens, came into view. We settled in a cottage within a few steps of the Pacific, where we could watch the sun dip below the horizon through waves which were often higher than our heads. By rented car, we explored all vantage points of the famed seventeen-mile drive. However, it was necessary to walk some distance through the almost sacred conservation area at Point Lobos to sketch the shore and those famous age-old cyprus trees, battered by onshore winds for hundreds of years; and of course we sketched the mission. The Spanish influence reminded her of Spain and a trip she had made there with her sister Ada.

In the evenings beside the log-burning fireplace, as we gazed through unusual portholes out of which we could see the Pacific, she would reminisce. She talked a little about the opposition and criticism she faced from friends. She was now far from the people who took exception to her mode of life and could allow her feelings to come to the surface. 'All our weaknesses and inheritances are known to the Almighty. Who are we to have such knowledge with which to judge others?'

Many of her friends were intolerant of any pattern of life that differed from their own – and Emily Warren's life differed widely. They wanted her to stop travelling and to conduct her life in what they considered a more businesslike way. 'My friends are pretty jealous and criticize me a good deal,' she told me. 'I think it pretty

---

7. This was the only occasion on which I knew Emily Warren to have a brand new outfit. The long black velvet dress that she wore to lecture in all the years I knew her must have been the grandmother of today's packable dresses.

cool. I told them if I could I should take them with me. You know I have a good many commissions to do, and it's not exactly play.'

It was difficult for Ottawa society to understand her. She explained to me that many of the women talked only about 'their children, their recipes and their frocks', and she had no time for that. 'Really, if you think too much about clothes you are nothing but a clothes peg.' Then too she was beginning to feel her years. 'Wicked waste of time is dreadful. I work harder all the time for, you see, I might get doddery. So long as one's mind is all right and knows everything, one is all right.'

To capture her thoughts, I kept my note pad by the kitchen door and, even though logs were expensive, made frequent trips to refuel the fire from the wood pile or to fetch a cup of tea. While she paused in reverie after reminiscing about Italy, I stirred the embers, replenished the fire and steeped the tea. By the time it was served she was back in England. 'And when you are telling it, you might mention the episode about my godmother and legacy; that would make a good story if we just twigged it a little,' she said with a mischievous twinkle in her eye. Before having our tea, we had a good laugh over my embarrassment at being discovered secretly taking down her words. She was entirely uninhibited and, I judged, pleased at having such a respectful listener.

She shared with me memories of her travels and the people she had seen. 'The simple English country people were so beauty-loving, but their weakness of today appalls me. The people in Spain, poor little things, are so dirty, not anything like the Italian people. They were on the brink of revolution when I was there. There was shooting a block from my hotel. But the amazing ones are the Irish people. On the Island of Achill you'll see a man in rags doff his hat and behave as if he were a count. "Pray be seated, ma'am, please come near the fire", in a filthy room with chickens, pigs and dirt everywhere. The Irish Free State is like that.' Again she recalled the quaint costumes of the Zuider Zee region, which she captured in paints before that part of Holland became more accessible: 'Those pretty Dutch caps with ears, the tight bodice, billowing skirt, wooden shoes; the men with high cap, short jacket, neck scarf and baggy pants.'

Emily Warren had firm critical ideas that led her to disapprove of much modern art. These criticisms came from her own belief in realist art as a universal language based on the universal presence of nature and of the basic elements of human civilization. She believed that inspired realist art could lead people to enjoy and profit by the beauty of the world, whether natural or manmade. Though Ruskin admitted abstraction and pure design in art, at least theoretically, Warren did not believe that a dismantling by the artist of the forms of nature could have the beneficial effect upon mental balance and the perception of truth that realist art could have. In the art gallery in Carmel that year, we happened to find an exhibition of Archipenko's work. I really expected that we should be asked to leave, as she exploded: 'I wonder that these people aren't ashamed to have that awful stuff in their gallery – bits of bodies cut up – and a professor at that – leading others to cut up bodies. How horrible!'

As we left, a wooden statue loomed up beside her in the garden. 'Let me hold on to that post. I'm afraid that old professor will come along and kill me! Excuse me for holding up one foot. People in Ottawa are used to it, and think of me as a sort of bird standing on one foot. On my way to the restaurant in Ottawa I have two stopping places to rest my leg – a bench in a garden, and a chair in a kind tailor's shop.'

The week in Carmel passed all too swiftly. Warren still had a commission at Jasper to think about. From San Francisco, where we saw another very interesting old mission, she took a plane to Victoria to visit her cousin while I continued by rail to Vancouver.

Meeting her there, I learned that she had received a very painful – and possibly dangerous – bump on her head while boarding an airport limousine. However, with no thought of letting that detain her, she entrained for Jasper, and I went with her. The weather was extremely cold and cloudy. The roads out of town were closed to motor vehicles, and her headache became worse. Yet, with the temperature minus $10°$F, she was able to plan her picture for the Canadian National Railway by sitting and memorizing her subject in a taxi on location for three-quarters of an hour. While she concentrated on the effects of the moonlight, not a word was spoken by driver or passengers.

The next morning was spent painting a sketch from memory of the mountain in moonlight. Then it seemed prudent to proceed to Winnipeg where damage, if any, could be discovered before she was due to leave for England. Her diary recorded 'no breakage'!

The medical examination and x-ray were overshadowed by a visit to the Winnipeg Art Gallery where she met the Canadian painter John Russell. He became very enthusiastic about her work and suggested to the curator that an exhibition should be held in Winnipeg the next fall. That made her feel much better, because it would provide an opportunity for the show about which she had dreamed for several years – 'The Cathedrals of Man and of Nature'. As it turned out, the completion of some of her cathedral drawings finally had to be abandoned: time was short, and there were too many interruptions. Thus the Winnipeg exhibition became another of her endeavours which failed to succeed.

CHAPTER VI

Fortunately I Can Still Work

The house may get a bit cronky but the mind of older people,
if kept alive, is the same.
EMILY WARREN, 1952

Emily Warren had lived with zest, finding no day long enough. She faced the difficulties of old age with the same spirit, but she bitterly resented the attitude of many towards the elderly. 'Canadians are cruel and the men are the worst. They persist in talking down to older people, especially women. You don't become wicked or silly because you are old.' She thought that she had missed chances for work because of this attitude.

By mid-1951, however, her physical stamina was beginning to show signs of wear and tear. Yet the same amount of production was needed to maintain her income. Conscientious friends who gave her commissions had no conception of the punishment taken to execute them. Part of the trouble was her own determination never to make mere copies of scenes she had already painted. Rather, she preferred to paint them again from nature (or the building in question) and produce a new, different interpretation – even if this meant making no profit. She spurned the idea of making copies: 'It is like dragging a golden ring in the dust,' she told me. If indisposition did result from overstraining herself to complete a commission, her own remedy of a few days by the sea or in the mountains usually proved to be a good cure.

London, July 12, 1951
I find London very disturbed and crowded – difficult to get any work done. Am at present at Ely. Have tried to do an interior but now, July 17th, am at Whitby for a few days getting some sea air.

Was blown out of Ely Minster; the Vergers would insist on having a big West door wide open and every door in the cathedral wide open both sides, so I decided it was not worth getting my neuritis and arthritis worse for the sake of one drawing, so I gave up and came here for a few days' sea air.

I next heard of her from Newfoundland.

Gander Airport, August 8, 1951
I meant to write before but was very busy before I left London
yesterday. Now have been delayed since early morning at this
airport on the way to St John's where I should have arrived this
morning. It is pouring rain and plane is cancelled probably on
account of fog over the sea ...

That gave her time to meditate and rearrange her schedule.

Am very seriously thinking of changing my place of residence in
Canada but I have lived so long in Ottawa. Many of my friends are
gone above, there still remain some who have become enemies!! I
really don't know what I've done. My first work must be to finish
four small water colours, the commissions, before I begin to prepare
for my Exhibition. Those things are part – a large part – of my
income.
    Alas! The cathedrals and mountain pictures will, I fear, never
sell. It's rather quixotic of me to try the cathedral show.
    It would be lovely to have another trip with you. It was so grand
when we were together at Carmel and Jasper. I have a picture to
paint for my transportation so it will be long after Christmas before
I get to cathedrals.

More than fifty drawings of cathedrals which had never been exhibited were discovered and photographed in 1978.
    I had arranged the year before for Emily Warren to give a lecture
at the Granite Club in Toronto that fall for a fee of $100.00. 'A
princely sum,' she called it, and decided to present her series on
England, which included Oxford, Cambridge, Windsor, Eton, and so
on. She was to lecture in the hall located next to the curling rink. On
12 November she wrote me about arrangements.

About the megaphone – in church rooms where acoustics were good,
I have often spoken to 500 or 600 people. Can you hire one? It was
at the Royal York for the English Speaking Union that I used one.
Perhaps at the Granite Club, I might be showing the Hathaway
Cottage interior, when 'sweep' is called. If so, that would be
appropriate.

I began to be somewhat worried about her ability to carry through an
assignment for which I felt responsible, but I received the following
reassurance: 'I am not the least bit uncalm; going steadily on as I
have also my own little exhibition starting here later this month.'
Knowing how weary she must be from the overnight trip by train and
the exertion of hanging the pictures, I asked if notes would help her
with her lecture. That was a blunder for she answered: 'Certainly

not, I know it as well as I know "me" prayers.' She spoke while seated, and to my relief she managed quite well. Several members followed her to the reception afterward and I thought they would never let her leave.

A few weeks later a puzzling and ambiguous letter showed deep concern about her financial state, though her sense of humour remained intact:

Ottawa, January 22, 1952

I began this a few days ago. Since then, have heard of the loss of a quite large sum of money which I had hoped would have paid for me when I am too old to work. Have been rather upset naturally. Have asked my lawyer about it and hope it will get settled satisfactorily but 'hae me doutes'.

Fortunately my eyesight is good and I can still work, but the left leg is almost paralyzed and I can't stand, though I can walk ... two or three miles. Nothing can be done for the injured leg ... boiling water went over it in 1936; I think I told you about it last year, but it's worse since then. My heart, in consequence of these shocks, is playing me up a bit – but I am not giving in and can do all sorts of things to keep up. These tumble [icy] roads make it almost impossible to get 'round so I am obliged to taxi if I have anything to do but – I don't, thank goodness, have to paint with my leg! Am not worrying, for I know the wonderful Father of all will help me too.

Am still hoping to have a show of interiors, etc. in Winnipeg, beginning in November, so must review the date with the Director of the Art Gallery there. Do you know his name? My brain seems to have gone pulpy a bit but in the main, is quite as clear as ever, only this has been a horrible shock.

Ottawa, February 4, 1952

... About the money loss, it will not affect me yet, perhaps not at all? If I just keep my sight and health and can get enough light to be able to see (nearly always it is too dark for that) ... The date we arranged last year when you came with me to the Art Gallery at Winnipeg and we saw the Director, was, I believe, November 10th or 16th. I am now quite well, really, 'spite of the tiresome left leg which doesn't really stop me in doing things.

Am going to Montreal soon to get a CPR transportation to do Mount Eisenhower on that line of route. Have roughly begun the CNR painting of Mount Pyramid and directly the light is better, will be working at the YW hall ...

She had planned a very brief visit to Toronto but was forced to cancel it, and I never solved the mystery of this loss of money. But it was a shock to one so determined to be independent.

Ottawa, Sunday, 1952
*Many thanks for your letter. I couldn't have come anyway for I am
far from well. It isn't flu but the result of two bad falls, one, the last
one, right near this door. Expect it was the ice which is so shocking
in the roads and even up all the steps. Though I take taxis all the
time, yet a fall often comes. The legal affair has resulted by arrangements being made – the creditors get one-third of the debts and will
be asked to forego any more money. I made enquiries through the
Crawley accountants here and also a man who has been my lawyer
for many years (made my Will, etc. some years ago).[1] A Will seems
a farce for me, but I suppose there will be a few pictures. Presently
I shall have the Old Age Pension! Have filled up papers about it.*

No Canadian ever deserved to receive that pension more than did
Emily Warren in 1952 at the age of eighty-two. It almost paid her
board and room the last four years of her life. Her next letter omitted
the date.

*Have had so many difficulties, bad weather, materials I got in
Newfoundland useless, and the oil mountain picture only just
started – three cathedral interiors all ruined by materials. I am
beginning or hoping to work on the fourth attempt later on. Also
haven't started on illustrations for my cousin's story!!! Sounds awful,
but do hope things will straighten out with better health. Light is
very good now but I simply cannot paint. My head got such bad
knocks. Much love to you, faithfullest friend of all, dearest C. ...*

This winter was proving to be desperately difficult for her, but she
still planned to go to England.

Ottawa, March 4, 1952
*Am so sorry to have been so long in answering. Have had a lot of
untoward things happen. This awful icy winter has caused me a
great deal of trouble – three bad falls on the back of my head. At
present am in a very small sort of convalescent home near the
research place in Ottawa. Have a very bad headache all the time and
shock to my system. When the least tired, great round lights, very
dazzling, surround my eyes all over. Also the doctor says my heart
has been a bit affected.*
*I've got tons of work to do so am hoping all will clear up. Am
flying to England March 31st. Three of my friends are helping me
a little toward this expense and I make up the rest, so the only thing*

---

1. She may have been referring to the sale of her house in England. Her
lawyer, Edwin H. Charleson of McNulty, Charleson, and Anglin, made
her will in 1948.

One of the two 'Canada's Tribute' paintings
(both oil on canvas, 717 x 168 cm) in the Hall of Fame,
Parliament Buildings, Ottawa, where it hung from 1941 to 1948.
The second painting was placed opposite.
Both are now at the Royal Military College, Kingston, Ontario.

Winter in the Gatineau.
c. 1940. 22 x 30 cm.
Courtesy of Mrs Lionel Dent, Ottawa.

is to live in hope. I had just started the CNR *Pyramid picture but can't do much until I am better. Also the Newfoundland cathedral pictures got completely ruined – three of them!! Am now planning to start the fourth. This terrible icy Winter is the cause of all my troubles. How are matters with you? My eyes are really very good ones, so the doctor said last year. Now, I nearly all the time, especially when tired, have dancing spots of white light all over them. Fortunately I managed to get all my things stored by the end of last week, so am resting a great deal and hoping for the best. Getting very tired so must stop.*

Later I received from the same address the following letter, unlike any that I had before; the writing was very irregular and the envelope had been crumpled:

March 14, 1952

Had a very bad fall in Ottawa on the back of my head. Cleared up my storage and am now in a sort of nursing home here but want to leave as soon as possible. Made a mistake in a little too much fox-glove stuff, but hope it will be all right. Hope to leave here tonight but phone the Hopes. Will tell you all about this unfortunate fall etc. Had a horrible time.

An overdose of digitalis? The thought alarmed me; the bad writing proved how ill she must have been. I went to Ottawa as quickly as possible.

Next morning, after an anxious night on the sleeper from Toronto, I inquired at 14 Thomas Street how the patient was getting along. Warren seemed to have been watching or listening because she heard my voice and came downstairs at once. She took me into the living room, closed the door, and ceremoniously waited until we were face to face. 'Am I crackers? Take a good look at me and tell me if I am crazy. People who come to visit say, "How she has been? Has she been wild again today?" I was so weak I could not cross the room without sitting down. They withheld my trays because I went out to post your letter. "You can't go out," she said. "You must not!" "But," I protested, "I am a free woman and have always made my own decisions." I knew things like this could happen in Russia but never thought it possible in Canada.'

Her alarm was so obvious, and I so shocked, that I suggested she leave at once. 'I have packed for I knew you would come and my rent is paid for a week in advance.' The taxi driver asked where to go, and until that moment I hadn't thought of anything but leaving. 'Where now?' I pondered. 'I know of a ski resort up in the Gatineau where I could rest until this crack on my head subsides,' she said.

Major Edgar K. Quip had a small hotel, Mountain Lodge, near

Kingsmere. We were his only guests, and though we arrived un-invited, he treated Emily Warren as if she were royalty. She found a spot just to her liking on an old-fashioned hard couch underneath the stairway to the second floor; during the day she lay there in the dark. The chef made up for those missed trays at the convalescent home, and in a few days she was ready for a short stroll out of doors in the snows of the Gatineau Hills. Then it came time to pack once more. She remarked, 'Life is not a matter so much of clothes, as it is of miscellaneous things.' So in went the mucilage, the ink, the dishes, cosmetics, laundry, gloves to sew, shoes, pictures half done and a few wearables, while out stayed the umbrella, sketching stool, and bulky roll of drawing paper. 'It's most dangerous these days to be alive,' she mused and really meant it.

Before starting off again for England, she consented to have an x-ray at a nearby hospital. We were driven by our host to the town of Wakefield, where we found the hospital in process of reconstruction, with noisy workmen, prodded by a worried-looking architect, wander-ing everywhere. Warren was given a bed beside a large plate glass window, a stool for climbing into bed, and an old lady for a com-panion.

Three days later the following telegram came to me in Toronto: 'Miss Warren unsuitable patient, must leave at once.' Naturally, any patient who puts an umbrella over her face in hospital would seem to be in the wrong institution; but I had seen her do it many times on our trip. She had a reason. 'My eyes like darkness. They have had much wear and tear from colouring lantern slides.' Moreover, I knew that she had a second reason – a jealously guarded secret. During the illness which followed the accident to her leg in 1936, she had lost her hair and thus had to wear a wig. Sick as she was, her pride would not allow the whispering gallery to learn of her loss of hair. The terror of detention from her recent experience in the con-valescent home may not have subsided and the slightest coercion would have met with defiance.

A friend removed her from hospital and two days later she was on her way to England.

Stratford-on-Avon, April 10, 1952
I meant to have written to you long ago – alas for good intentions!
At the moment I am in Stratford-on-Avon, had terrible difficulty to find a place to stop, but have a little bedroom here with breakfast. It's very cold, such a strong, cold wind. Am not feeling at all well. There is a wide-spread epidemic of sore throat and cough, so I have picked it up but when it warms up a bit, I'll be better.

My bumped head still bothers me a good deal, but, of course, it's bound to take some time to get rid of it – or rather of the bumped feeling!

Bossons Glacier and the Matterhorn, Switzerland.
1911. 40 x 28 cm.
Private collection.

St. Mark's Cathedral, Venice, at Fiesta.
c. 1911. 36 x 58 cm.
Private collection.

London, May 7, 1952
It is very wet and cold over here and it makes it so difficult to get all
my work done. Have been paying a few short visits to old friends and
resting a good deal to get my head well more quickly. Am going to
Windsor July and August so I hope the weather will be better then.
The bluebells will be coming into bloom at Kew and the rhododen-
drons also ...

Windsor, August 10, 1952
I am staying at the YW here at Windsor until 18th August when I
go to GFS, then leave by air September 1st. Crowds are so large, it is
almost impossible to draw or do anything in St. George's Chapel
and only get less than an hour a day.

She returned to Ottawa in September and had great difficulty finding
a room. 'Have got a temporary shelter – most uncomfortable room the
size of a pillbox and with no door.' She talked of taking an office for
a month so that she could finish the Mount Pyramid picture she had
to do for the CNR. In October she again sketched the autumn colours
in the Gatineau.

Ottawa, October 8, 1952
I would like so much to have a few sheets of that art paper. Will you
please be so kind as to ring up the dealer and ask him to send me
four sheets and I will at once send the money directly I know how
much it will be.
*   The tints are coming along now and I shall be going up the*
Gatineau Saturday, the only day one can get coaches. Am afraid I
shall not get to Meach Lake to stop there because the Hopes are
coming in almost immediately, but I shall go to Kingsmere and places
where I can get to [by bus]. I am fearfully behind in my work but I
am much better. It must be laziness and old age coming on. Haven't
done the picture for CNR yet but am very comfortable here with a
good light and a nice landlady – very different type.

I had persuaded her to see Dr F. Carlyle Hamilton, a Toronto
cardiologist, when she had been visiting me not long before. His
advice to me had been to allow her freedom to go where she wished
and do as she thought best, advice quite contrary to the restraint that
friends in Ottawa were trying to impose. Certainly her frequent
troubles were quite a burden to them as she grew older; and as many
of her friends predeceased her, strangers who did not understand
joined the parley. The sad part was that no one, anywhere, fathomed
her dreadful fear of indigence and confinement.
    In November she had her customary annual show at the Children's
Library and then she had to move again because her room could not

be heated properly. In January she came to Toronto to speak at the Royal York Hotel to the Business and Professional Women's Club of Toronto on Scandinavia. Then she went to Eastern Canada for four lectures beginning on 11 February at Halifax.

> *The Lord Nelson,*
> *Halifax*
> *February 11, 1953*
> *Am afraid I did a great deal toward making you tired. Did so much enjoy seeing you again. The journey was quite comfortable and I appreciated and enjoyed the lunch you gave me very much. The hot coffee did me a great deal of good for the train was very cold and I was near the door which opened onto the platform. Thought I was getting the grippe but warded it off. Now resting a bit. This is a lovely hotel, right on the port.*

The lectures in the Maritimes to the Canadian Clubs were her last public appearances on the platform. She spoke on one of the seventeen different subjects which for thirty years had delighted Canadian audiences from coast to coast. Illustrations for these included more than nineteen hundred hand-coloured slides of her own paintings. The *London Free Press* reported one of her early lectures to the Women's Canadian Club.

> *Emily M.B. Warren ... lectured last night to a charmed audience ... and again on this, her fourth or fifth appearance in London within a few years, amazed her public by her industry and her gifts.*
>
> *Miss Warren is one of the most faithful and constant devotees of art the era has produced. That she should turn out so great a volume of work with no lessening of merit is in itself notable. On each of her previous visits to London she came equipped with an extensive array of slides, taken from her own paintings and covering widely varying fields of art.*[2]

The lantern slides (and the sketches and paintings from which they were taken) represent the major exception to the absence of the human figure in Warren's work. She painted few figures, basically because she disliked doing genre painting, though she introduced them where appropriate, as in 'Canada's Tribute'. But in her lectures she loved to explain colourful customs and legends of the places she had visited, and her lantern slides often showed people at their daily work or traditional recreations.

---

2. *London Free Press*, 23 March 1928.

Ruskin's unfinished sketch of Milan Cathedral,
given to Emily Warren and used in her lectures on Ruskin.

Street in Neuchâtel, Switzerland.
Date unknown. 33 x 13 cm.
Courtesy of Mrs Helen Simpson Lynett, Toronto.

CHAPTER VII

Last Years

Ah! the souls of those that die are but the sunbeams
lifted higher.
EMILY WARREN, 1955

After spending the summer of 1953 abroad, Emily Warren firmly objected to living in any private house, probably because the terror of possible strict confinement still lingered. Unfortunately the kind of accommodation for which she was looking was simply not available. She took a room in the Bytown Inn but it was not long before the management appealed to her friends to have her placed elsewhere; since she was now 83 years old they did not consider her sufficiently responsible to be in their hotel. The following description, by one of her admirers, might illustrate why the hotel management was reluctant to have her. 'Outwardly, as I knew her, she was a rather dowdy old lady with a somewhat obvious wig, often slightly askew on her head, clothes mostly dark and drab, with an indifferent cardigan to protect her from the elements, a dark floppy old hat whenever she was outside painting on location.'

The matter of housing became critical. A letter from one of her friends stated: 'The possibilities are that she cannot keep this going for more than a matter of weeks. Friends are helpless ...' In fact well-meaning friends tried to prevent her from taking such extravagant accommodation. To one who chastised her for travelling so far she answered, 'You mean stay home? I couldn't be bothered! I've no time to be a little old lady.' She left Ottawa abruptly, and moved to a rooming house in Montreal which was close to the bus station and the YWCA. Soon her money dwindled more rapidly, not because of the cost of the room (a very high $4.00 per night), but because it evidently was stolen. Mrs John Hope, of the Hope's Book Store, Ottawa, who never failed to give her refuge, would see her off by bus for Montreal with $100 in her purse, then within a few days she would be back for more. About this time the Bank of Montreal was then instructed, apparently by someone who had gained authority over her financial affairs, to give her merely a subsistence allowance.

During a visit that winter I found her in a small single room, the only window of which faced a brick wall. She was extremely weak

and having trouble with her feet. In order to dine at the Laurentian
Hotel one block distant, it was necessary to take her by taxi. Even
then, she required rest before returning to her rooming house. One
had to feel sorry for her as she deliberated: 'I'm not a bit nervous, but
"me" leg is – If I get tired it gets wobbly. They told me the blood
doesn't get to it very much. It's black, you know, as black as a stove.'

With the arrival of spring she began to feel somewhat better and
the perennial urge to go abroad returned. On my way to Montreal at
the beginning of June to see my daughter embark for Europe, I
happened to pass through Ottawa and there learned that Warren had
just left Canada. Knowing how frail she had been, I checked with the
Montreal landlady. It was no surprise to hear that, at first, Warren expected to go but, on the day before flight time she felt much too ill so
she changed her mind. According to Mrs Archambeault, her landlady, Warren only had the ticket for her eastbound flight. An attend-
ant from the airline came to the house saying that he had instructions to make sure she got on the plane for that certain flight. He did
just that.

A little later, I bade farewell to my daughter and her friend, two
young music students bound for Europe, and prayed that somehow,
somewhere in England they might find Emily Warren. As soon as
their ship reached Liverpool, they hastened to London and began a
search. Warren's friends there had not heard from her. The Girls'
Friendly Society reported that she had indeed arrived, but with no
reservation had been turned away. After some explanation and
persuasion, the Bank of Montreal, her usual address in London,
finally admitted that she had been in to withdraw the balance of her
account. They also suggested checking with BOAC. There it was confirmed that 'Miss Emily Warren' had flown immediately back to
Canada. Had she slept or had a meal during that shortest of thirty
visits to Europe? In any case, she returned to the Montreal rooming
house.

Meanwhile, the search for a solution to this problem of finding
suitable accommodation continued. At last, someone found a
pleasant spot just seventeen miles from Ottawa at Dunrobin where
she could be well cared for. The 'autumn tints', which beckoned her
back to Canada each year, gave her a friendly greeting as she arrived
at the home of Mrs Daisy Kennedy, a registered nurse who soon
came to be called her 'guardian angel'. Although living on a farm was
lonely for one used to the bustle of cities, Warren was sensible
enough to realize that her strength was waning and she was in need
of good food and rest.

The surroundings at this pleasant farmhouse, therefore, were just
what she needed. To roam out of doors at will made her feel like a
bird out of a cage. The Kennedy grandchildren who wandered in and

out became an absorbing interest. At other times she had the company of successive families of kittens which proved to be as fond of her as she was of them. During one of my visits, as she held one on her knee, she remarked: 'I had a vision the other day of going to Heaven, but they wouldn't let me in. As I was turning away I heard a faint meow from my beloved Freddie. Then the gates opened and I went in to join him.

'You must not worry about me, my dear, for I shall know when my life is coming to an end, so, why should I fear until then?'

When the colours were at their best, Mrs Kennedy gave her opportunities to sketch by the shores of the Ottawa River but that skill seemed to have left her. At the house she busied herself trying to improve old drawings, either by trimming them to a size which seemed to make a better composition, or by trying to touch them up, only to make them 'no good'. That was her common expression if her work displeased her. However, each day her paints were moistened and prepared for work, so that she at least felt busy and planned 'a show much later on'.

Early in 1956, false rumours that she was bankrupt began to circulate amongst Social Service personnel in Ottawa. News came to me that they were considering the Perley Home for elderly persons as a suitable shelter for Emily Warren. Indeed, she herself may have sensed something of the kind when she requested Mrs Kennedy to bring her a statement from the bank in Ottawa. They showed it to me and she had a sizeable balance, over $6,200, which would have kept her for years. As her pension almost covered the price of her board and there were practically no other expenses, Mrs Kennedy and I were at a loss to understand what was going on or who was responsible for such rumours. To forestall any plan to move her, and also to provide her with ready cash, I hastily arranged for a sale of seven of the cathedral paintings. Naturally, Warren found it rather puzzling to understand such sudden interest in her large paintings, which had been exhibited so many times without a single sale. At one time in her life, she had intended to bequeath the collection of forty-five to the National Trust in Great Britain because half of those churches were either damaged or demolished in the bombings. When the Labour government, of which she did not approve, came into power, however, she had a change of heart; the works remained in storage year after year and now she could no longer go to Ottawa to enjoy seeing them. Even so, she hesitated to part with them until it was carefully explained that they would be going to friends for her benefit.

One night in December 1955 she felt well enough to attend a farewell party given by the congregation of the local church for their minister. With such a stimulus and a minimum of prompting she was able to give an enjoyable slide show as the entertainment of the evening. But her recovery was short-lived. After the confinement of the winter months there was a noticeable decline. On one occasion as we were chatting in the early spring she made a solemn gesture pointing her thumb toward the ground and calmly remarked, 'I shall soon be down there, I know now ... but in the meantime I have these lovely little friends – darling children and pussies.'[1]

About a month later I saw her lying helpless, her circulation very poor, yet she spoke to me as naturally as ever before. According to Mrs Kennedy, Warren's mind wandered at times into realms of imagination as she would study the trees coming into bud and address them as if talking to old friends, which, of course, they were. Her sincere love of beauty, which she had shown first by drawing flowers constantly during childhood, had developed into what finally became her main purpose in life. She longed to have her fellow Canadians share that love. Just as Ruskin, through his books, opened the eyes of his countrymen to wonders never before dreamed of, Emily Warren, his youngest disciple, laboured literally day and night for over three decades to do likewise for her fellow Canadians.

The true personality of Emily Warren was summed up in a friend's lovely eulogy, after the painter had died quietly in her sleep from natural causes at Dunrobin on 28 June 1956, in her eighty-seventh year. 'It saddens me to think that I could not have seen more of her during the last few years for I loved her as I never loved another; not only for her gift in art, much as I appreciated that, but for the utter Christliness of her character. The aroma of that sweet flower benefited all who came within its radius.'

----

1. Warren had previously selected a site for her grave to face the sunset in Springhill Cemetery at Vernon near Ottawa. On the grounds of this peaceful spot there is a chapel which, before restoration, was a country schoolhouse. Behind the lectern her friend Dr Lorne MacLachlan, DDS, has set up a memorial consisting of the reproductions of her two masterpieces, 'Canada's Tribute', and a watercolour of Westminster Abbey above a bronze plaque. Other homelike furnishings make this room a shrine for all those who knew Emily Warren.

'An Out-door Oven, Richelieu Valley'.
From *The Spell of French Canada* by Frank Oliver Call, 1926.
As with many of the paintings for *Homes and Haunts of John Ruskin*,
the original for the colour lithograph book illustration reproduced here
has not been located.

The octogenarian with 'no time to be a little old lady', c. 1950.

CHAPTER VIII

Emily Warren, the Painter

... the truth of nature is part of the truth of God; to him
who does not search it out, darkness,
as it is to him who does, infinity.
JOHN RUSKIN, 1888

The two decades from 1919 to 1939 were the period of Emily Warren's greatest productivity in Canada. From 1940, the remaining 16 years of her life yielded many paintings that show her talent in its full vigour, but these years were increasingly filled with physical ailments, family responsibilities, and financial struggle. Toward the end there was also Warren's preoccupation with maintaining her independence in the face of well-wishers, some of them perhaps misdirected, who at times suggested placing her in nursing homes or taking control of her affairs. But during the twenties and thirties she was at the height of her powers and relatively free from the many cares that increasingly beset her and would have overwhelmed a less powerful and cheerful character.

Excellent paintings flowed from Emily Warren in a steady stream during these two decades. She produced hundreds – perhaps thousands – of works, including watercolours, oils and sketches. Besides, she illustrated her lectures with over nineteen hundred lantern slides reproduced from her paintings. She made these tiny squares of glass into an art form of her own: many of them, still preserved, are incredibly delicate miniatures which, when projected, glow with an added dimension of the inner light that was a hallmark of the Warren style.

Her large output resulted in an important body of Canadian work unique not only for its own qualities but for its historical ties to Ruskin and the 'impressionism' he championed (though he later failed to recognize it in the Impressionists themselves). In conclusion, then, we should try to see Emily Warren's work in terms of the ideas and the rich tradition that fed it.

Under Ruskin's guidance, she devoted herself to developing a technique that could reveal the divine, sacramental gift of goodness and strength, which the English critic-philosopher saw in nature and in the great works of human creativity. At a comparatively early age, probably in her mid-twenties, she achieved a mature style which served to express her ideas and to treat her favourite – her obsessive – subjects. This style varied little throughout the remainder of her life. From that point forward her development occurred not so much in artistic technique as in understanding of the world around her. She was a tireless student of geography, geology, architecture and art. She travelled widely and had an omnivorous appetite for new landscapes, human types, styles of dress and domestic architecture, natural hues and forms. The colours of Canada's eastern forests – and, at a later date, the Rocky Mountains – struck her with great force, the force of a revelation, and she never ceased to discover and be stirred by new facets of their beauty.

Her main subjects can be divided into three large groups: landscapes, architecture and a loose category that would include scenes more intimate and humble than the others: gardens, village streets, people engaged in common tasks or pursuits traditional to their cultures. The first two categories, landscapes and architecture, include the bulk of her major work; and under these headings, her most characteristic paintings were mountainscapes and cathedrals. She saw a profound connection between these two phenomena, as shown by her plan for an exhibit on the subject, 'Cathedrals of Man and of Nature'. Though her paintings often depicted monumental scenes and expressed emotions of power and 'sublimity', as that concept was defined in the eighteenth and nineteenth centuries, she managed also to convey a humaneness, even a friendliness, that emanated from nature and the great works of civilization.

In one of her treatments of the 'sublime' in architecture, she shows a portion of the interior of Chartres Cathedral, looking along the ambulatory with its long rows of columns and huge volumes. The scene is suffused by light that radiates from the stained glass windows and softens without removing the detail. The major architectural masses, such as pillars, and even the surface detail of their decorations, are clearly rendered in the foreground. But the whole composition seems to escape the boundaries of what can be seen, both at the edges of the frame and in the shadowy recesses of the background. The perfect proportions of masses and spaces which Warren has shown extend indefinitely into areas that cannot be seen. In this way the painting suggests the true immensity of the cathedral – the infinity which the building itself was meant to evoke and which the painting can only hint at. Into this scene Warren has introduced two human figures. They might have been dwarfed by the building: almost inevitably, it would seem, their presence must give an impression of mankind's smallness before the great works of the past. However, the painting blends them with the same light and shadow, the same harmony and play of colours, which create Warren's vision of the cathedral itself, so that they seem natural, comfortable, welcome inhabitants there. They are not insensitive to the infinity of the

The Strand Looking East, London.
1921. 21 x 17½ cm.
Showing the Law Courts and the Griffin
that marked the boundary of the Old City of London.
Warren's sketch of the arch that stood over the statue is on the reverse.
Private collection.

Vicar's Close, Wells Cathedral, England.
c. 1940. 23 x 30 cm.
Courtesy of Mrs Gerald Collyer, London, Ontario.

cathedral, but they are not oppressed by it or irrelevant to it, either.

Few of Emily Warren's paintings of cathedrals and churches – in fact, few of her architectural paintings in general – are mere studies of buildings or portions of buildings. Not that she was imprecise in her handling of these subjects. She paid careful attention to full presentation not only of form and colour but of specific detail. True to Ruskin's principles, she always conveyed in her compositions exactly the way in which the eye perceives much detail close up and gradually, at increased distances, loses the ability to distinguish the exact nature of detail though not the perception that detail is *there* (this characteristic of vision is carefully analyzed by Ruskin in *Modern Painters*, Vol. I, Part 2, Sec. 2, Chap. 5).

But in addition to objective detail and the way in which a piece of architecture actually strikes the eye, Warren was always interested in the meaning and emotion conveyed by buildings, both through their historic and legendary associations, and especially through their own statements as works of art. Her architectural paintings form her dialogue with the great artists of the past, and give her a place as an important interpreter of late medieval and Renaissance architecture in Western Europe and England. She was well suited to such a task, no doubt, by an inner sympathy. For though she was not a theorist, she had been formed by Ruskin's views, views toward which she was inclined even before meeting him by her religion, her early education and her sensitivity to the temper of her times. And Ruskin's belief in the duty of great art to convey and interpret the glory of God in a profound sense, truly didactic but not narrowly so, was a living link to the ideas and ideals that had also motivated earlier Christian and Christian humanist artists.

Emily Warren's treatment of nature, also, can be illuminated by reference to Ruskin's theories, which go beyond technical and aesthetic theories to place painting in a larger philosophy of nature and of human psychology. The basic tenet of Ruskin's view is one that places him as firmly within the tradition of Wordsworth as many modern painters are within the tradition of Freud. Ruskin believed that the eye, when it actually *sees* anything, is creative, cooperating with nature. He further believed that the human eye and perceptions are naturally prodded toward creative vision by the beauty providentially placed in nature, and by man's own animal appetite and love for visual experience. The painter's task is to educate his eye and refine his sensibilities. And the function of painting itself is to perform this education.

Near the beginning of *Modern Painters*, Ruskin comments: '... my first business ... must be to combat the nearly universal error of belief among the thoughtless and unreflecting, that they know what nature is, or what is like her; that they can discover truth by instinct ... I have to prove to them ... that the truth of nature is part of the truth of

God; to him who does not search it out, darkness, as it is to him who does, infinity.' This was the basis of the education that *Modern Painters* was intended to give the public, and it is the basis of the education Ruskin himself gave Emily Warren.

Painting, in Ruskin's view, is based on a kind of creative perception. It springs from an inborn 'acuteness of bodily sense' and a love for things that is a holy and universal force, shared in common by nature, man and God. In the same way, Wordsworth in 1798 had spoken of himself as a lover of

> *... all the mighty world*
> *Of eye, and ear, – both what they half create,*
> *And what perceive; well pleased to recognise*
> *In nature and the language of the sense*
> *The anchor of my purest thoughts, the nurse,*
> *The guide, the guardian of my heart, and soul*
> *Of all my moral being.*
> (*'Lines Composed a Few Miles Above Tintern Abbey'*, 105–111)

This view of Wordsworth's and Ruskin's was not a doctrine of slavish imitation of nature. Rather, it was a rebirth of the Renaissance view of art in its original strength and fullness; it required a loving investigation of and respect for nature as a divine symbol. At the same time, it added a new Romantic emphasis upon the creative role of man. It saw man's power to perceive truth and create art as a spark of divinity given especially to the human spirit; it was this spark that cooperated with nature to *create* the world in which man really lived: the world within his imagination, expressed by his art.

In Emily Warren's paintings and in her whole attitude to art, we find this belief that the painter creates the scene, both with his eye and his mind. But at the same time, he does not wholly create it, but cooperates with a truth present in nature, and therefore he must be faithful to the object before him. Like her architectural paintings, her landscapes faithfully represent the scenes she painted, but are nothing at all like photographic representations. They always intend primarily to give the feeling of the scene. And in Warren's paintings, this feeling is almost always one of joy, either a calm and humble joy as in her village and garden scenes, or a sublime but nonetheless humane joy, as in her mountainscapes. Though she did innumerable landscapes during her long and active career, and sometimes painted the same scene several times, nearly every painting is distinct. It is as though her goal were to portray the infinite variations nature plays on this basic fact of joy.

There is an important wholeness and similarity between any of her individual paintings taken singly and her career taken as a whole.

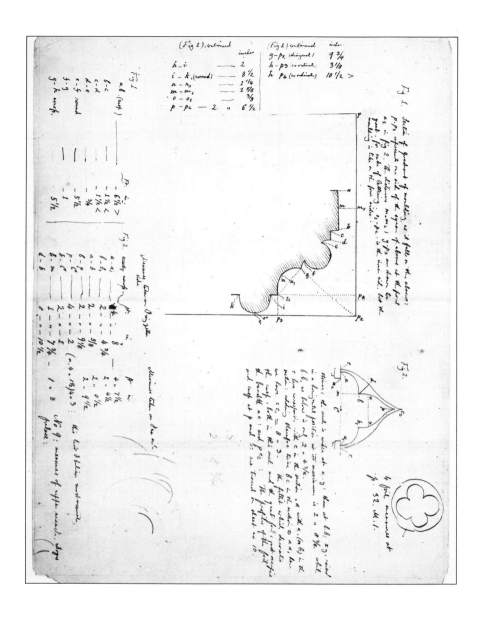

A Ruskin 'teaching' drawing,
one of several which belonged to Emily Warren.
Courtesy of Thomas Fisher Rare Book Library, University of Toronto.

John Ruskin's Study.
1916. 22 x 17 cm.
One of a pair of paintings that together
show almost the whole interior of the room.
Private collection.
Photograph by Avo Koplimae.

In each painting, she tried to grasp and convey the forms of nature that lay beneath the shifting appearances, and the whole body of her painting does the same on a larger scale. Her major landscapes concentrate on mountains or other large views, often involving lakes and almost always forests, meadows and similar areas of verdure. It may be said that, what Turner was to the sea and the atmosphere, Emily Warren tried to be to the contours of the earth and to the green world. Though not as great or original a painter as Turner, she succeeded in no small measure. Commenting on Turner's treatment of water, Ruskin defines his genius by contrasting him with the vague impressions of water that most other artists usually give:

A little crumbling white, or lightly rubbed paper, will soon give the effect of indiscriminate foam; but nature gives more than foam, she shows beneath it, and through it, a peculiar character of exquisitely studied form bestowed on every wave and line of fall: and it is this variety of definite character which Turner always aims at, rejecting, as much as possible, everything that conceals or overwhelms it.
(Modern Painters, Vol. I, Part 2, Sec. 5, Chap. 3)

In the same way, Warren sought to show the clear forms that lie beneath the restless detail of nature. She knew that the natural details she loved, and the play of light and colour which was her constant theme, were expressions of 'this variety of definite character' which is the basic truth of any landscape. Each of her paintings delights in the unique surface of the landscape it portrays, yet at the same time each feels for the inner form. And her work as a whole performs the same labour.

It will be obvious to anyone looking at Warren's paintings for the first time that her greatest strength is the representation of light and colour. Her work has strong similarities to Impressionism, though there is no evidence that the Impressionists influenced her. It is more likely that, under Ruskin's guidance, she developed independently in a parallel direction. In all her painting, there is virtually no use of primary colours. She laid on her watercolours and mixed her oils to provide a high degree of transparency, so that her scenes often seem to glow; light not only falls on them, but fills them and radiates from them. Light gives each scene its colours and surface moulding, and actually provides its form as well. This is in accord with Ruskin's theories of the way in which the educated eye imparts love and veneration – the 'moral sensations' – to what it sees, and thus works with nature to create the imaginative universe in which we live. Light is the medium of the eye, in which it acts. And light is also the element of visual imagination: the painter's element. Emily Warren, as a painter, lived in and through light; and her paintings express the way in which the very forms of nature come to us as shapes of light and colour.

The mission of praise which was Warren's career as a painter doubtless sustained her in the often difficult circumstances of her life. After coming to Canada, her lack of acceptance among this country's exhibiting artists forced her to travel in order to do commission paintings and to lecture. This pattern tended to steadily increase her isolation from the art establishment at the same time that it brought her into wide contact with ordinary people who appreciated her art, certainly, but in many cases were not able to see its true stature. This situation, which might have meant only drudgery and bitterness to many other painters, she took in stride, and even embraced, as an opportunity to bring the 'religion of beauty' to people. The economic necessity that forced her to paint constantly, and often to paint what others ordered from her, she transformed into a source of further accomplishment.

The religion of beauty, the attempt to lead a large public to find love and joy in sacramental nature, is not an idea of current art, which tends to emphasize inner turmoil and the unknowableness of the world. But this Victorian concept does not, on the other hand, ignore problems. Respect for it, and sympathetic interpretation of it, have increased as our own century has outgrown the need to reject its Romantic and Victorian parentage. It is likely, therefore, that Warren's painting too will undergo a sympathetic reappraisal.

Warren, like Ruskin, was fully aware of the pain and struggle of human life, in society and within the individual. She met economic and social injustice, prejudice and physical illness head on throughout her life, and fought them both for herself and others. But like Ruskin, she emphasized not the analysis of human weakness but its healing through access to a sacred realm that was offered to human beings and placed within their grasp. Her own attitude is well expressed by the words of her great teacher in his 'Epilogue' to the final edition of *Modern Painters*. The passage is dated 'Sunday, September 16th, 1888' by Ruskin, and thus was written almost exactly five years after his first letter to Emily Warren, and during the period when he was instructing her:

All that is involved in these passionate utterances of my youth was ... concentrated into the aphorism ..., 'All great Art is Praise'.

Appendix A

In 1917 while painting interiors of Westminster Abbey, I observed the placing of the Colours of a Canadian Regiment on Wolfe's Monument. This scene I reproduced in oils, and it was purchased by Dr Doughty, Dominion Archivist, for the Canadian Archives where the painting is now hanging. A colour reproduction is attached.

At that time the idea was conceived of a symbolic painting to portray Canada's Tribute to the First World War. I pursued this work in closest cooperation with the London Office of the Canadian War Records, and under the inspiration and encouragement of the distinguished persons who appear in the paintings. With the exception of His Royal Highness, the Prince of Wales, and Major General M.S. Mercer, CB, all persons in the paintings posed for their portraits, enabling me to complete the work.

His Excellency The Duke of Connaught visited the Abbey and gave me his personal assistance, not only by posing for his portrait, but in helping me place the individuals in proper order of rank.

My conception of the work to be created was expanded under the advice of the senior officers who co-operated in the production of these paintings. It necessitated trips to various military depots in the United Kingdom, in working out a schedule of appointments with the persons included in the groups. Models were hired to pose the different positions of individuals in the group, uniforms had to be purchased, and of course the outlay for canvas, oils, transportation of the paintings from the United Kingdom to Canada, all of which amounted to an expenditure of at least Five Thousand Dollars.

I was led to believe on a number of occasions that a commission would be arranged assigning me the task of completing these oils for the Canadian War Records Committee. Mr Paul Konody, Art Advisor to the Canadian War Records Committee, visited me while painting in the Abbey and discussed the matter fully. The fact remains that no commission was given before the funds of the Canadian War Records Committee for this purpose were closed.

The war came to an end before I had completed my paintings. Sir Arthur Currie prevailed upon me to bring these oils to Canada, and finish them in Ottawa by painting in the remaining persons whom I had not been able to pose in London. This fact has been confirmed by Colonel H. Willis-O'Connor, Aide de Camp to Sir Arthur at the time.

Upon completion of the work, June 8, 1920, the late Sir Robert Borden, then Prime Minister, requested me to address a communication to him offering the two paintings to the government for the total sum of Ten Thousand Dollars. I dictated my offer to a member of the staff, and addressed the signed proposal to the Prime Minister. On the instructions of the Prime Minister, the paintings were hung in the Reading Room of the House of Commons, pending the completion of the purchase. Sir Robert Borden's illness intervened, and the negotiations were never completed.

In 1927 a group of Members of the House of Commons including Messrs Winkler, Mackenzie (of Neepawa) and Thorson (now Mr Justice Thorson) discussed my paintings, and I was informed at that time they were confident of arrangements being made for the government to purchase them.

I should explain that during the years from 1920-1939 I travelled to Europe each year and continued painting subjects of my choice and under commission, both in European countries and the British Isles. In 1939 I found myself in Canada and unable to return to Britain.

In 1941 through the assistance of Dr Beauchesne and the courtesy of the Speaker of the House of Commons, my paintings were placed in the Hall of Fame in the Parliament Buildings where they are now hanging.

I understand that in 1944 the status of my paintings was again discussed with Messrs Winkler and Mackenzie (of Neepawa), when attempts were made to have the paintings presented to either McGill University or the University of British Columbia, through the patronage of some individual. I understand that one deterrent to completing such a plan has been the question of doubt raised in the minds of those to whom the proposal was made, as to why these paintings which have been considered of sufficient merit to appear prominently in the Hall of Fame subject to the review of thousands of people during the war years, have not been acquired by the government.

These paintings were conceived as symbolic works, and are therefore of historical rather than artistic value. Consequently I have understood the reasons why they are not items which might be acquired by the National Art Gallery, although I understand they were referred to a Committee of the Art Gallery and refused.

Last spring I was compelled to leave Canada by airplane to attend the deathbed of my sister, and to arrange the details of an impoverished estate. During my absence I understand my paintings were again the subject of discussion among some Members of Parliament. After my return from Britain in October I was informed that arrangements were again being considered to have the paintings purchased for the House of Commons, and since that time I have been hoping that the plan would materialize.

Last week I was advised by Dr Beauchesne that provision could not be made to have the paintings purchased, and that I would have to accept responsibility for them being transferred to some other location of my choice.

EMILY M.B. WARREN
March 1, 1947

Appendix B

On 13 May 1949, Charles A. Bowman, retired editor of the Ottawa *Evening Citizen*, published the following account of the long 'Canada's Tribute' affair as Chapter 27 of his continuing retrospective series, 'Through The Citizen's Looking Glass'.

WAR PAINTINGS FINALLY MADE HALL OF FAME
Sir Robert Borden wanted the government to purchase Miss E.M.B. Warren's war memorial paintings, but he had resigned; and the new Conservative administration would do nothing to meet his wishes. He enlisted the interest of The Citizen.

After carrying the burden through the stress of war years, the state of Sir Robert Borden's health impelled him to resign as prime minister in 1920. The Union government had disintegrated. Mr Crerar, one of the Liberal members of the coalition cabinet, resigned first. Mr Calder went to the Senate. Liberal members like Dr Michael Clark moved back to the opposition side of the House. Sir Robert made way for Mr Arthur Meighen to become prime minister.

I had been invited to see Miss Warren's paintings – of the Canadian colours deposited on Wolfe's monument in Westminster Abbey. At Sir Arthur Currie's invitation, she had brought the large oil paintings from England, to be finished in Ottawa. A workroom had been allotted to her in the Museum Building – where parliament met after fire destroyed the buildings on Parliament Hill.

* * *

Miss Warren, a pupil of John Ruskin's, told me how she had been inspired to start this monumental work – without realizing the magnitude of it. Under Ruskin's influence, she had studied architecture, and painted for preference in British and European cathedrals. During the war, after Vimy and other Canadian battles, she happened to be working in Westminster Abbey, at her easel set up near Wolfe's Monument.

Canadian regimental colours had been deposited everywhere on the monument, for safe keeping while the troops were in the trenches across the Channel. Canadian soldiers on furlough would come to visit the Abbey. Sometimes they would attend morning service.

Miss Warren decided to paint 'Canada's Tribute'. Day after day, soldiers would stand by her easel to watch the progress of the painting. They would lay particular stress on the desirability of a prominent place in the picture for their regimental flag. There were so many flags to be shown, she finally found it necessary to paint twin pictures on two large canvas sheets.

Miss Warren made the mistake, however, of paying heed to too many advisers. They wanted figures painted into the picture – Sir Arthur Currie, the Canadian commander-in-chief; the Prince of Wales, Sir Robert Borden – until finally she had an assembly of soldiers and statesmen painted in, around the foot of the monument.

Generals and other high-ranking officers would come to her studio, to have their portraits painted for the flag scene. The war ended before she could get the paintings finished. So she brought the large canvasses to Ottawa.

Sir Robert Borden told me he regarded Miss Warren's paintings of national historical interest. He had fully intended that an item should be put into the estimates, to purchase them for the nation. But Sir Robert had resigned before the necessary provision could be made.

He felt the position to be embarrassing – as he had been painted into the picture as a central figure. He approved, however, when I offered to interview Mr Meighen on the matter. But Mr Meighen had other things to think about: he simply passed me on to the new minister of public works, Mr F.B. McCurdy.

A shrewd, calculating trader, Mr McCurdy restrained himself from asking how much I expected to make out of the sale of the pictures to the government; but he proceeded to mention a monetary valuation – much below the artist's price – in which I had no interest in any case.

Sir Robert had authorized me to say that he hoped the government would buy the pictures, but that made no difference. Doubtless in party politics, as in other competitive fields, it is: 'The king is dead; long live the king!'

My next approach was to the board of directors of the National Art Gallery, at that time presided over by Sir Edmund Byron Walker. The Gallery took the position, quite properly, that they were the trustees of public expenditure on meritorious works of art. They had very limited funds, and could not be influenced by any political or sentimental consideration.

When I submitted that Sir Robert Borden as prime minister had intended that they should be purchased with a special vote, and still wished it, Sir Edmund took the view that, under such circumstances, a moral obligation perhaps rested on the government ... but the Gallery could do nothing about it.

*   *   *

So the war memorial paintings were housed for several months in *The Citizen* building – in Mr H.S. Southam's office, although he had profoundly different tastes in art. Later they were moved to Trafalgar House, the Canadian Legion clubhouse on Cartier street and very nearly lost in a fire. They were carried across to Sir Henry Egan's house by GWVA rescuers, including Grant McNeil and George Herwig.

How they peregrinated to Moyse Hall, at McGill – where Sir Arthur Currie equally desired with Sir Robert that they should become national property – and to Sir James MacBrien's office at RCMP headquarters is a long story. A committee of three members of parliament, Col Cyrus W. Peck, VC, Major G.W. Andrews, DSO, and Major Hume Cronyn, tried in vain to interest Mr Meighen's administration.

In later years, when it seemed desirable that surviving ex-soldiers in parliament should have first-hand knowledge of Sir Robert Borden's interest in the paintings, he very kindly and cordially agreed to meet some of my Liberal acquaintances. Messrs J.T. Thorson (now judge of the Exchequer Court), Howard Winkler and F.D. Mackenzie (Neepawa) were invited to tea at Sir Robert's House. They came away impressed with the veteran statesman's kindliness and sincerity.

Happily, through the good offices of Mr Arthur Beauchesne, Clerk of the House, and other officials of good will on Parliament Hill, Miss Warren's paintings were hung where they could be seen by members of parliament and the public, in the Hall of Fame.

After many years, a disinterested and devoted champion of justice, Mr Clive Planta – national secretary of the Fisheries Council of Canada – took up the cause. He succeeded, greatly to the satisfaction of many disinterested people and admirers of Miss Warren's work in Ottawa. It is to the lasting credit of Mr Mackenzie King, while still prime minister, that the memorial paintings were finally purchased – and Sir Robert Borden's cherished wish consummated.

Cenotaph, London.
c. 1921. 23 x 17 cm.
This picture expresses Emily Warren's devotion to the memory
of the dead of two wars, and her message of comfort to the bereaved.
Courtesy of Mr Paul Hoskins, Renfrew, Ontario.

LECTURES

By
E. M. B. WARREN, R.B.A.

1. **Homes and Haunts of Great Men.**
   Shakespeare, Milton, Dickens, Wordsworth, Scott, Carlyle and others.

2. **London—its Interests and Beauties.**
   The places always seen by overseas visitors, as well as many others not so well known. London is shown from dawn to dusk.

3. **John Ruskin—His Life and Work, Homes and Haunts.**
   Being a personal friend as a little girl during Ruskin's last years Miss Warren is able to give many interesting reminiscences unpublished before. Besides lantern pictures, some of Ruskin's unpublished letters and original drawings are shown.

4. **English Cathedrals.**
   Their Architecture. History and Legends popularly told.

5. **Historic Spots.**
   Windsor and Eton, Oxford and Cambridge, Boston, Canterbury, etc.

6. **Through the Land of Heather.**
   An illustrated ramble through the Border Country to Edinburgh, Glasgow, the Trossachs, etc., to the Highlands and the North of Scotland.

7. **Famous Cities of Romance.**
   Paris, Rome, Florence and Venice, etc.

8. **The Playground of Europe.**
   Rambles through Switzerland; its historic as well as its beauty spots.

(P.T.O.)

---

9. **Here and There in France.**
   Normandy, Brittany, The Riviera, etc.

10. **The Charm of England.**
    Rural scenes, old customs, etc., as well as its old world towns and buildings.

11. **Wanderings through Holland and Belgium.**

12. **The Charm of Gardens.**
    Their charm in History and Legend from earliest days in England and elsewhere, flower and plant legends, etc.

13. **The Emerald Isle.**
    i.e., Ireland. Its beauty spots, legends and charm.

14. **The Land of the Maple.**
    Canada from Coast to Coast; its history and beauty spots, etc.

15. **Rambles in Spain.**
    From the Basque Country to Madrid, Seville, Granada, etc.

16. **Scandinavia.**
    The Lands of Peace: Denmark, Sweden, Norway—from end to end.

17. **Beautiful Italy.**
    The charm of its Scenery, Architecture, History, etc., from North to South.

All 17 Lectures are illustrated by the Lecturer's Painted Slides, taken from her own original Water Colour Pictures, painted on the spots.

Address—
September to end of March:
81 Laurier Avenue West, Ottawa, Canada

April to September:
"Rosemary," West Clandon, Surrey, England.

Emily Warren's lecture programme, 1939.

Bibliography

The main collection of materials relating to E.M.B. Warren and her work is now deposited at the Thomas Fisher Rare Book Library at the University of Toronto. It consists of:

Copies of three letters and a telegram from John Ruskin.
 Three samples of Ruskin's teaching drawings.
 Emily Warren's 18-page treatise on Ruskin and her description of his study.
 A photocopy of the file of newspaper clippings relating to Emily Warren that was collected by the National Gallery, Ottawa, from 1920 until her death in 1956.
 A pair of rare coloured reproductions made by the Montreal Gazette in 1921 of 'Canada's Tribute'.
 A bound volume containing copies of letters written by Emily Warren to Constance McRae from 1928 to 1954.
 Sixteen hundred hand-painted lantern slides which Emily Warren used to illustrate her lectures on seventeen subjects.

The Canadian War Museum, Ottawa, holds watercolour sketches of all the regimental flags which were done in preparation for painting them in 'Canada's Tribute', as well as portrait sketches of Sir Robert Borden and Padre Canon Scott. The 11′ × 6′ 'Canada's Tribute' canvasses are in Currie Hall, Royal Military College, Kingston, Ontario.

A coloured film catalogue of Warren paintings is in preparation and will eventually be deposited in the Thomas Fisher Rare Book Library. As of November 1980 about a thousand Warren paintings have been located in Canada and the majority of them have been photographed for the catalogue. Sixty of her 165 recorded studies of cathedrals in Europe and Canada are included; practically all of these are in watercolour. Illustrations by Emily Warren appear in the following books:

E.T. Cook, Homes and Haunts of John Ruskin *(London: George Allen & Co., 1912) includes 28 in colour and 16 in black and white. Frank Oliver Call,* The Spell of French Canada *(Boston: L.C. Page, 1926) includes 3 illustrations in colour.*
– The Spell of Acadia *(Boston: L.C. Page, 1930). Frontispiece in colour.*

Her work was also represented on Raphael Tuck & Sons postcards.
   In addition to the many newspaper reports of her activities that are preserved in the National Gallery file, articles on E. Warren appear in the following:

Queen, the Lady's Newspaper *(London), 2 September 1905.*
National Life *(New York), November 1921.*
Saturday Night *(Toronto), 4 December 1920.*
Canadian Collector Magazine *(Toronto), November-December, 1977.*
Antiques & Art *(Vancouver), June-July, 1980.*

The following reference books include entries for her:

Who's Who in Art *(London, 1934)*
Benezit's dictionary of painters, sculptors, drawers, and engravers, *vol. 8 (Paris, 1948).*
Who's Who, *1955 (London, 1955).*
Allgemeines Lexikon der Bildenden Kunstler von der Antike bis zur Gegenwart *(Leipzig, c. 1942; updated by Hans Vollmer, 1961).*
Royal Society of British Artists: Members Exhibiting *1931-1946 (Leigh-on-Sea, England, 1976).*